YOUR PURPOSE IS YOUR SUPERPOWER

Discover Your Life's Assignment and Become A Powerful You

From Best Selling Author

HENRY L. RAZOR

S.H.E. PUBLISHING, LLC

DEDICATION

This book is dedicated to my grandchildren Lyric Razor, Liberty Razor, Lake Razor, Lennard Razor Jr., and Aubrey Tyms! You guys are my motivation to fulfill my purpose so that the world that you inherit is the optimal place for you all to fulfill your purposes.

YOU GUYS ARE AWESOME!

SUPERPOWER

noun

a power or ability of the kind possessed by superheroes: a superhuman power

ACKNOWLEDGEMENTS

First, I give thanks to God for His direction and guidance while preparing this work for distribution.

To my wife, Janette, who was very patient with me during this project I say 'Honey, I thank you so much.

To the leadership team at The Faith Place-Chicago, you guys are one in a million and your commitment to the success of this ministry with perfection is unmatched.

I must acknowledge Michelle Hudson for the brilliant cover design

And to the entire Faith Hope & Charity Church family, I thank God for you all being such a loving church. You all are, without doubt, THE GREATEST CHURCH IN THE WORLD!

Pastor Henry L. Razor

FOREWORD by Dawn Callahan

I posted a flyer on my social media platforms advertising a free, marketing course I teach at the college. The flyer has a QR code that requires a smartphone to scan and it will go to the registration page. Because I understand most people will see this flyer on their cell phones, I also posted a registration link. It was live on the platforms for just a few minutes before someone said, 'Can you please provide a link so I can register because I'm on my cell phone and can't use the QR code?' I thought for a second, maybe I forgot to post the link so I went back to check and it was there. Then, I clicked on it to make sure it worked. It worked. I went back to the comment and mentioned that the link was in the text above and returned to my other tasks. Again, I received a notification of a new comment. The same person went on to say that I was not understanding their question. They had clicked on the link and there was no place to register. I thought for a second before I realized the issue.

The registration button was not in its usual place on the registration page, and one had to do something different to find it. It required a change in behavior. I didn't think to explain this because I assumed that if someone was interested enough to click on the link, that same interest would compel them to find a way to register. But I was mistaken. I was asking them to do something that they don't normally do, and that is to have definiteness of purpose. In his book Outwitting the Devil, Napoleon Hill gives us seven principles to overcome the devil and his wicked ways. The first principle, definiteness of purpose, states that once you decide on a purpose, you must go after it with everything you have and don't stop until it is accomplished. This task can often stop us in our tracks and indirectly become a multi-generational behavior. Children learn first from the people they see on a regular basis, and let's face it, most of us don't embrace change gracefully. We tend to resist, kick, and scream, frustrated that we have to learn something new after finally finding comfort in what we know to be true. We seldom consider 1 that what we know may not be as clear-cut as we thought. And when we are told of additional information, all we hear is blame, shame, guilt, and frustration. Therefore, it's no wonder why God chose Pastor Henry Razor, who possesses a rare quality in pastoral ministry to take a deep dive into the Word and go into covenant with Him to ensure that he is meeting his congregation where they are and tailoring his teachings to invoke the change needed to enjoy their promised birthrights. This is crucial because it requires a shift in behavior and a definiteness of purpose that many people struggle with. By tailoring his teachings to meet his congregation where they are and helping them to understand the importance of their purpose, Pastor Razor is doing a great service to all who encounter his teachings.

Introducing the concept of leaning into your purpose and understanding your power is not a common practice in modern society. Since we do not openly discuss our purpose, we tend to expect or hope to discover it comfortably, in line with the plans we have for our lives, without fully comprehending or questioning our responsibility in seeking our purpose. As children, we often assume that being an adult means automatically knowing why we are here, but in reality, many adults have no idea what their purpose is. Since it's not a topic we typically discuss on a regular basis, we may go through life without ever questioning it.

The first time I heard about pursuing a purpose was when I came across the popular book, The Purpose Driven Life, by Rick Warren. Even then, I didn't feel compelled to read it. I saw the title and thought, "That's interesting," before moving on. When I was growing up, my parents had their own ideas about what I would become when I grew up. They thought I would make a good lawyer because I was always asking "why" and loved reading. When I started babysitting in the neighborhood, they thought I would make an excellent pediatrician. And when my grades began to slip in high school, they simply hoped I would graduate. But none of these suggestions were based on my passions or interests.

As I reflect on my past, I realize that the expectations my family had for me were not based on our conversations. I remember telling my dad that I wanted to be an artist, but he discouraged me, saying that artists only receive recognition after they have passed away. The truth is, I asked "why" so often because I felt that I deserved to know everything. I only babysat to get out of the house, and I struggled to focus on my studies because I was constantly worried about a bully who had singled me out. We often choose our career paths based on practical considerations, such as providing for ourselves and our families, rather than pursuing our passions. Many people work in professions that were chosen for them by their parents or that provide the right title and income, or simply work a job to keep food on the table.

In addition, the role of the church and our understanding of our purpose has been a complex and challenging relationship. The Christian church has been historically patriarchal, and as society's traditional norms continue to shift, it becomes even more complicated. Although I wasn't required to attend church every Sunday, I did attend frequently enough to have found church homes throughout my childhood and adulthood. I participated in occasional Bible studies, youth events, and revivals. The messages that resonated with me were often those that instilled fear of damnation, emphasized service to God and our neighbors, and listed countless "don'ts." However, it was the "don'ts" that caused a tumultuous relationship with God. Whenever I felt like I had messed up, the guilt was enough to make me think, "Why bother? You're not going to be what is preached." This didn't leave much room to consider my passion or my purpose.

I recall the moment when I walked away from Christianity. As a little girl, I had a lot of questions, but I wasn't receiving the answers I was looking for. I also wasn't actively seeking answers, but I knew that I wasn't living the way I had been taught, which would result in eternal punishment. One day, while in my car, I had a conversation with God. I expressed my uncertainty about Christianity and let Him know that I was going to explore other religions. I made a promise that if I didn't find anything that resonated with me, I would return to Christianity. God, being the loving Father He is, blessed me with free will and allowed me to make my own choices.

I won't bore you with the details of my life before I found my way back to God, but I will tell you this: when I returned home, there was no judgment, no shame, and no condemnation - certainly not the kind I would have faced from people if I had walked away from the church for as long as I did from God. God knew the whole time where I was and He waited patiently as I tried to navigate life without His guidance. He knew I couldn't make it on my own, but He also knew why I ended up where I did and never once turned His back on me. It was all a part of the plan. As I slowly made my way back into His loving arms, I remember the day I cried out to Him, desperate for an understanding of my purpose and why I was here. I felt like I was behind and wanted to make up for the lost time. Dear, your purpose is your life. The journey. With or without me was never in vain.

From that conversation on, I understood that my life up to that point was all part of His Master plan. I wasn't behind. Quite the opposite. I was right on time. And so are you.

Life will take you on a wild ride, full of ups and downs, joy and pain, fear and shame. But through it all, remember that everything happens for a reason. You may look back and see mistakes, but God sees you as you are now - molded into the person with the unique abilities to fulfill your role in His master plan. This book was written for you to read at this point in your life. You have the ability to lean into your purpose, but it's important to understand that you were chosen. You're exactly where you're supposed to be. So, embrace this journey with an open heart and mind, and trust in God, knowing you can't get it wrong.

Have you ever heard the saying, "Favor ain't fair"? What is considered fair in the eyes of God and the eyes of man are made up of so many differences that I am not qualified to list them all. However, what I do know is that God does not make mistakes. Let this book serve as one of many tools that you can use to seek and fully understand your purpose.

As you read, it can be helpful to have your Bible nearby and to look up each verse to ensure that you fully understand the message. It's also important to pray and meditate on the words as you relate each chapter to your own life. Keep in mind that you may not know everything, and that's okay. It's important to approach your journey with the innocence and imagination of a child, so that God can lead you and provide guidance in ways that only He can. Trust in His plan and allow Him to work in your life as you study and grow in His word.

PREFACE

In the fall of 2022, I was lead of the Spirit to create a workshop and deliver it to my church. The workshop would be about divine purpose and it would include much needed guidance on understanding, identifying and fulfilling one's Gods issued assignment.

Being obedient, I scheduled the workshop and over the course of the next few weeks, I sought God as to just what I was going to be teaching. My mind was opened to the reality of purpose and my understanding of each individual's plan within God's master plan became ever so clear. I obediently conducted the workshop and afterwards packed my materials, thinking that was the end of it.

Then, on the second Sunday in March, I was sitting in our worship service and I heard the spirit say "teach the people how to defeat the enemies of purpose." So I commenced praying for the content to teach, and God, being faithful, responded by giving me three lessons. While teaching these lessons, I was instructed to add these lessons to the content from the workshop and publish it. And this book is the result.

This book is for everyone that has ever lived. It defines personal Divine Purpose relative to God's master plan for the world, provides inspired procedures for identify your purpose, gives biblical guidance on defeating the enemies of your purpose, and encourages and motivates you to fulfill your purpose. This book, with its accompanying workbook, represents God's design for you to live your very best life by doing what you were created to do.

TABLE OF CONTENTS

INTRODUCTION

From the very first days of humanity, man has expended an enormous amount of personal time and energy toiling to make this world the best place possible to reside. We are always creating, designing, developing, inventing, adjusting, modifying, etc., with the hope that the results of our labors will in some way assist us in our duties as the keepers of this earth. We spend an enormous amount of time trying to achieve personal success that aligns with the success of the universe. We have come to realize that it is within this global alignment that the very crux of our existence dwells.

But achieving this alignment is not as uncomplicated as it would seem to appear. Life itself presents numerous challenges; and we are daily faced with opposing forces, opposition that's at work against us, opposition that's working to resist the peace and harmony for which we so relentlessly labor. Sometimes, with all that we do to reach that place of inner peace, joy, and harmony, with ourselves first, then the world around us, it appears as if the world is just not cooperating. And when we are not in harmony with the world around us, the world can be a very cold and lonely place.

It is when we find ourselves in a place where it seems as if it is us against the world that we begin to ask ourselves questions. And normally these are questions for which we have no answer, for if the answers were already with us, we would not have allowed ourselves to be in a cold lonely place. These cold and lonely times in our lives have triggers. They are triggered when we experience failure in projects, or experience broken relationships, have dysfunction in family, stagnation in career, etc., and many other missteps in our journey to the blissful life that we strive to obtain. And when these triggers are released, instead of enjoying life, we find ourselves trying to figure out what is wrong, or what went wrong, or where did things fall apart, etc. Then with each non answer to these questions, we see ourselves moving further away from the happiness goal that we have set for ourselves, and deeper into the coldness of a lonely world.

It is in these times that it appears that we are not synchronized with the world. For all that it's worth; it's as if the world is actually working against us, working to bring about our failure. We've followed all of the rules, made the correct choices, dotted every "I" and crossed every "T", but things still are not working out. We seem to be failing, even though we are doing the exact same things that we've witnessed others experience success doing. Our inability to tap into that positive energy is enough to turn our perplexity into despair.

Then finally we arrive at the question that is at the core of our perplexed state. The question for which, if we only knew the answer, would allow us to exit the unhappy place and walk in life's harmony and success. And that question:

Why am I here on earth anyway?

This is the question that has perplexed millions of people throughout generations, even from the creation of man.

Anyone who has ever accomplished anything or achieved any level of success has asked this question of themselves; but more importantly, the people who achieve success in life and accomplish great things have had to arrive at an answer to this question. And not just an answer, but the correct answer, because until you reach the destination where the correct answer resides, you will be continually investing your energy without a positive return on your investment. And failure to produce a positive return on your investment of energy almost always leads to frustration and despair. And, oh, it must be noted that the correct answer to that question is very different for each individual. There are numerous variables that must be considered when attempting to determine just why you were placed on earth. But the constant drain of your energy, when you are attempting to be successful not knowing why you are even here, will negatively impact you emotionally, it will consume large amounts of your time, it will deprive you of your inner peace, and it will propel you to a place of hopelessness. And this place of hopelessness is not a desirable place to be. This is the place that you wish to avoid; but if you find that you've already landed in this place, it must become a place where your exit becomes your first and foremost priority. So it is imperative that you arrive at the correct answer to this question!

Avoiding the inherent hopelessness of not knowing the answer to the 'why' of your existence, or leaving this place of hopelessness after you realize that you're there, occurs only when you understand who you are, why you are, and what you should be doing with your life.

The pages of the book will provide instruction and guidance to assist you in arriving at the correct answer to the question, why you were placed on earth. And once you have this knowledge, you will be encouraged and motivated to live your best life and complete the assignment for which you were placed on earth to fulfill.

As a pastor, I am often confronted with questions about personal life purpose. These are questions for which I answer with prayer, knowledge, learning, concern, and personal experience. There is no 'one size fits all' answer to questions about personal life purpose. We are all different individuals, with specific personal skills, very different personal life experiences, different knowledge areas, etc., and so are our life purposes and life assignments will be very different and uniquely specific. But our God is one Lord[1] and He has only one plan for the entirety of humanity. AND YOUR PURPOSE FITS WITHIN HIS PLAN! The Bible clearly states that all humanity is one,[2] as a people. But this one *humanity* consists of multiple distinct individuals, each having a specific and personal assignment that, when combined the assignment of others, makes us a single harmoniously functioning entity.

This book represents the next phase of a period of divine guidance and instruction that God has directed me to deliver to His people. I commonly refer to this series of guidance and instruction tools as the '**Power of You for Successful Living**' series. This started when I was inspired to teach the '*Warring in the Spirit*' workshop at the church

---

[1] Mark 12:29
[2] Galatians 3:28

where I serve as senior pastor. The workshop was so powerful and the results that the participants experienced were so astonishing and profound, that many of the participants demanded that I place this information in book form. This resulted in me writing the first book in this series entitled '*Winning Spiritual Wars*'. This book went global and to this day I am receiving reports of supernatural victories as the content and message of the book is implemented. Then shortly thereafter, I was guided by the Spirit to write a follow-up booklet entitled '*The 4 Principles of Dominion Authority*'. This booklet too, went global and resulted in the *Exercising Dominion* workshop and an annual **Dominion Impact Conference**. Numerous people globally have now learned how to make winning a repeatable process that becomes a way of life. This is exactly how God purposed us to live. Then the next phase in the **Power of You for Successful Living** series had me teaching believers how to discover their Divine Purposes and fulfill them by conducting a '*Discovering Your Life's Purpose*' workshop. This workshop gave guidance and instruction on discovering your life's purpose. After delivering this workshop and receiving numerous testimonies of clarity, victory, and life elevation, I was divinely inspired to write this book, entitled '*Your Purpose Is Your Superpower.*' Then as I studied for a presentation that I had to make, I became enlightened as to how each of these workshops and books were actually connected and interrelated in a way that allows everyone to live life at the level for which they were purposed. This series of books, conferences, and workshops all represent a path to successful living, and a victorious life. So with the

5

publishing of this book, the **'Power of You for Successful Living'** series will consist of:

- **Winning Spiritual Wars** – *Book*
- **Warring In the Spirit** – *Workshop*
- **4 Principles of Dominion Authority** – *Book*
- **Exercising Dominion Authority** – *Workshop*
- **Discovering Your Life's Purpose** – *Workshop*
- **Your Purpose is Your Super Power** – *Book*
- **Dominion Impact Conference** – *Annual Conference*

Each book, conference, and workshop in this series is more than just something I've learned while studying, or something that I've heard or seen. Each unit in '**Power of You for Successful Living'** series is something that I've lived. I have personal experience applying the content and message of these book, conferences, and workshops in my life. I was born in a small rural town in Arkansas, in the Mississippi Delta region of the United States. I had fourteen siblings and we were poor, really poor. In the delta region at that time, cotton was king, so as a child I have permanent memories of working in the cotton fields. So I started implementing the principles of '**The Power of You for Successful Living'** series in my life at a very early age, even before I realized what I was doing. (*In this book, I explain how God directs us unbeknownst to us*). I started applying these principles, even when these principles were not being taught or understood by those in leadership at the church. And just as God is faithful, these principles elevated my life. These principles catapulted me from

6

picking and chopping cotton as a little kid, to a global technology Subject Matter Expert (SME); a position that saw me rise to global manager, with 13-18 of the most technical engineers in the world reporting to me; on 5 of the world's 7 continents. These principles elevated me from the fields of Arkansas to a prestigious career in the most technical industry in the world. And these principles will have the same effect on you.

Each of the books listed are currently available globally, and the workshops can be requested at the Faith Place Bible Institute website, www.fpbi.net. I don't know if, or when I will be directed or inspired to write additional books or develop additional workshops for this series, but I will remain in submission to God while remaining prayerful, so that if I am inspired to continue with this series, I will be ready and able.

I pray that this book brings clarity to your life, encourage and motivate you to fulfill your purpose, and provides you with the confidence to experience the successes and victories that come when you live life as God has purposed for you! I pray that this book empowers you to live your very best life!

**NOTE*: In this book I use the words' purpose, assignment, Divine Purpose, and Divine Assignment interchangeably. They all represent the same thing. They are divine because of who issued them.*

7

WHAT IS PURPOSE

PURPOSE

noun
noun: **purpose**; plural noun: **purposes**

the reason for which something is done or
created or for which something exists

Everyone has a reason for living. There is a specific reason
that every person was allocated space on this earth and
within the universe. God created all of us as ***living souls[3]***,
and He created us to execute a plan that He already had
established for the world at creation. Therefore, as living
souls that are created in the image of God, we are birthed
into this world with assigned individual functions that fits
into God's plan, and improves the world in which we live.
It is imperative that every living individual realize that God
created this world[4]; we must also realize that God made,
then populated this earth with us[5], and that He has a very

---

[3] Winning Spiritual Wars
[4] Isaiah 45:18
[5] Psalms 24:1; Isaiah 44:24

8

specific plan for all of His creation[6]. That's right; we are ALL placed on this earth **by God** for a specific work (***purpose***) as He establishes His kingdom on earth like it is in Heaven. Your individual life purpose is the assignment that God gave to you; and that assignment fits within God's overall plan for this world much like a piece of a puzzle. And just like the puzzle, any single piece that's missing, makes the puzzle incomplete. So your assignment is critical, crucial, and necessary within God's plan for the world.

Keep in mind that as created beings, our knowledge of God's complete plan is very limited[7]. Although we have the Bible as a document that reveals much about God, His creation, and the requirements for His created beings, we must also acknowledge and accept that there is so very much that we do not know. After all, God is sovereign in His authority and power, thereby permitting Him to do with His creation as He pleases[8]. He has declared that all humanity was created for their individual specific purposes[9]. And since our individual specific purposes are uniquely assigned to complete God's overall plan, then God's design for us as His creation causes our individual assignments to be inter-related in such ways that together they bring about the precise execution of God's master plan; His plan for all humanity. And don't ever get it twisted; God's master plan will succeed!

---

[6] Jeremiah 29:11
[7] 1 Corinthians 2:16
[8] Psalm 135:5-6
[9] Proverbs 16:4

9

Purpose provides us with the reason that God placed us here on earth. This reason should be a motivational asset for us as we journey through life. Having purpose should bring joy to you, knowing that your creator has implemented a plan with a specific assignment for you. There are things in life that only you are assigned to do. And when you consider the enormity of the world through generations and time, and consider that this entire world is included in His plan, and within that entire world you have a specific assignment, or role to play in its success, you should be overcome with emotion that God thought so much of you as an individual! Think about it, your assignment is a piece of God's puzzle, and this puzzle can't be complete without you!

HOW YOU FIT INTO GOD'S MASTERPLAN

God has a master plan, and He has offered you a strategic role to play in bringing about the success of this plan. Even beyond that, He displayed His wisdom and foreknowledge when He assigned this role to you, even before you were birthed into this world[10].

Because your purpose is such a critical part of God's master plan, you become empowered once you begin fulfilling it. This empowerment is because the master plan cannot fail, and since your purpose is a part of the master plan, you too, cannot fail. When you are fulfilling your purpose, the power that works in you comes directly from God. This God sourced power works through you to bring about the successful fulfillment of your purpose. This God sourced empowerment of you is why your purpose is your superpower! The Apostle Paul put it this way:

> *"Now unto him that is able to do exceeding abundantly above all that we ask or think, according to the power that worketh in us"*
> **Ephesians 3:20**

Because God's master plan will not fail, you must not fail in your purpose. While fulfilling your purpose, there will be times in your life when you are faced with situations and circumstances that require much more ability, power, and

---

[10] Isaiah 49:1; Ephesians 4:1

strength than you could possibly provide. In these times God has committed to intervening and doing more for you than you ask Him to do; He has committed to doing even more for you than you could even think that he'd do. And he's going to do it through you. THIS IS YOUR SUPERPOWER AT WORK!

God's master plan is so important within the structure of the world, that when you're fulfilling your purpose, failure is NOT even an option. You are given access to this tremendous power to ensure that you succeed. To understand the big picture, you must first gain proper perspective of God's master plan.

When I consider God's master plan, I can't help but recall my years in corporate America. I was trained and educated in the tech industry. In my professional tech career, I traveled to many places in the world supporting many of the most advanced data, audio, and video networks in utilization today. So let me take a moment or two, and create a paradigm of God's master plan, using the tech industry for which I was a part of for so many years.

Using the tech industry as my example, God is the Project Manager for. In corporate, a Project Manager would be defined as a professional who organizes, plans, and executes projects while working within restraints like budgets and schedules[11]". These professionals "are organized, goal-oriented professionals who use passion, creativity, and collaboration to design projects that are

---

[11] Coursera -- https://www.coursera.org/articles/what-is-project-manager

12

destined for success[12]. Let me make a point of clarity, I am not saying that God is a Project Manager, because God's power, roles, and responsibilities extend well beyond that of a Project Manager. God is the Supreme Being to whom we owe our very existence, and to whom the entirety of the universe must acknowledge and submit. But because of the roles and responsibilities of a Project Manager, I am drawing this comparison for ease of understanding and relevance.

For any project, the Project Manager must first know the desired end result that's expected at the completion of the project. In other words, the Project Manager must know the intended outcome for the project. And it is the knowledge of this desired output that the Project Manager uses to set individual and team goals, make individual and team assignments, create relevant timelines, and set expectations. The Project Manager must know what the completed puzzle should look like so that he/she can make the assignments that will most effectively and efficiently brings the pieces of the puzzle together. So God, just as a good Project Manager would, knows just how He wants His kingdom on earth to be established. When the disciples asked Jesus to teach them how to pray, He instructed them to pray that God's kingdom on earth be established just like His kingdom in heaven[13]. And since it's the objective of God's plan to set up His kingdom on earth, then He makes assignments to individuals based on His expected outcome, a divine kingdom on earth. And just as a Project Manager

---

[12] Project Management Institute -- https://www.pmi.org/about/learn-about-pmi/who-are-project-managers
[13] Matthew 6:10

considers the relevant qualifications of individuals and teams, then makes the assignment based on the most qualified match for the need, so has God done likewise when making His assignments. He has assigned to each of us unique individual roles in His kingdom here on earth. Your Divine Assignment is both unique and specific for you[14]. This is why you are much different from others. You are uniquely qualified to complete your assignment! You should celebrate your uniqueness because this difference is the reason why God graced you with the assignment that you have. It is also the reason for your empowerment.

Another major responsibility of a Project Manager is to ensure that everyone with assignments on the project is equipped with adequate and the correct resources needed to successfully perform their duties within the project. If they need a specific tool, it's the Project Manager's responsibility to make sure that they get it. If they need more resources, the Project Manager is responsible for providing them access to these needed resources. If more time is needed for a specific function, the Project Manager also manages the project timeline; therefore he/she simply makes time adjustments. This is how God relates to us relative to our purpose in life. It has been stated that "God does not call the qualified; but rather He qualifies those that He has called". While it is indeed true that God qualifies each and every individual to whom He makes assignments, (*and we will see later that this means everyone, the entirety of humanity*) we must accept this statement with the knowledge that the divine qualification process that God

---

[14] Jeremiah 29:11

uses begins long before we are even birthed into this world[15]. God brought you into the world with the abilities to successfully fulfill your purpose. He qualified you for your purpose even before you were born. An example of God's pre-birth selection process can be seen with Rebekah during the birth of the twins Jacob and Esau[16]. The Apostle Paul emphasized that God made His selection of, and hence His assignment to, Jacob before he was born. The selection wasn't because Jacob was righteous and Esau was evil, because Paul also emphasized that neither Jacob nor Esau had done anything right or wrong; but the sovereign God, who knew His master plan's outcome; He also gave both Jacob and Esau their abilities before birth, so He made assignments to each as such. There will be more on this later in this book.

Another major responsibility of the Project Manager is to create and maintain the inter-relationships between the diverse entities that have responsibilities within the project. This is where communications become the skill of importance, and the Project Manager must utilize this skill with precise attention to detail. God's plan for the world is a big plan that involves numerous people of every language, nationality, and region across the earth. In addition to everyone that currently populates this earth; God's plan also includes everyone that has ever lived, as well as everyone that will ever live. Only God can keep His master project in sync and keep the many diverse entities progressing towards a successful completion. He can do

---

[15] Ephesians 1:4
[16] Romans 9:10-13

this because He has created every person as a body, soul, and spirit. And the soul, which is a part of each of us, is what connects us to God and makes us all His children. And He has declared unequivocally that all souls belong to Him.[17] So via the soul He can guide us, give us unctions, give us dreams, give us intuitions, and even speak to us to inform us of His desires for us. And since He is managing the entire project, He also does likewise to the others who have assignments within His project; and when everyone follows His counsel and instruction, there is no conflict, friction, or overlap in responsibilities[18]. (*For an understanding of how the soul relates to the spirit and the body, pick up a copy of the book 'Winning Spiritual Wars'*) When we function in the area for which we have been given our Divine Assignment, or Divine Purpose (*Remember, I will use Divine Assignment and Divine Purpose interchangeably throughout this book, and at times I will simply say assignment or purpose*), we don't compete with each other, but rather we acquire understanding of how the assignments of others complement and enhance our work, and vice-versa. When we arrive at this realization and acquire this knowledge, we can celebrate the successes of others; knowing that we are all working on the same project and reporting up to the same Project Manager. When you succeed, the project is lifted and moved even closer to its successful completion. When others succeed, the project is also lifted and moved even closer to its successful completion. If we fulfill our own individual purposes, while working together as one

---

[17] Ezekiel 18:4
[18] Romans 8:16

harmonious unit[19], the master plan is successfully completed. This is why networking with other professions is so important! You should view those that you partner with while fulfilling your purpose to be the pieces of the puzzle that are adjacent to you.

Your purpose requires faith and commitment. Your faith must be established in two areas.

1. You must have faith in the Purpose Giver
2. You must have faith in yourself.

Faith in the Purpose Giver is a requirement, if for no other reason, than without it, you won't commit or give your all to something or someone in whom you have no confidence. It is a requirement that you believe in God if you are to walk in your purpose and fulfill your assignment on this earth. Putting this in a plain and simple statement, you must have faith in God[20]. But we should also acknowledge that believing in God takes on many different forms. You may not show your belief in the same manner as I, and you may not worship in the same ways as I; but the requirement is NOT for us to be the same, or to be as if we were cloned; the requirement is for us to have this belief in God as the Supreme Being, the Higher Power. If you are sincere in your belief, God will direct and guide you into the correct path for you,[21] and when considering the paths that we must take to fulfill our purpose, one size certainly does not fit all.

---

[19] Galatians 3:28
[20] Hebrews 11:6
[21] Proverbs 3:6

Along with your belief in God, faith in yourself is also a requirement if you are to fulfill your Divine Purpose. Just like the little engine that could, you have to be convinced that you can do this. It's not that you are elevating yourself or displaying the arrogant pride that is the forerunner of destruction,[22] but you must display the self-confidence of one who understands the authority that God has given to you as a living soul. So, ultimately, your confidence is really in the ability that you have acquired through God; It's confidence in *__the power that worketh__* in you. When working in the area of your Divine Purpose, you should always declare that you can accomplish anything because of this power that works in you.[23] This powerful declaration should be a staple for any and every area of your life.

Along with faith, you must have commitment and determination to successfully fulfill your purpose. There is a nugget of advice that I constantly tell myself when times get hard and the way ahead appears to be littered with concealed dangers, but I know that I must keep moving forward. I tell myself that anything that's worth having is worth fighting for. The rewards that are promised to me upon successful completion of my assignment definitely make my fight to fulfill it my purpose worth it. I will expound on the enemies of purpose that makes fighting for completion a requirement later in this book.

---

[22] Proverbs 16:18
[23] Philippians 4:13

So as I close the first chapter of this book, there are a few take-a-ways that you need to retain as you read further in this book.

1. You have a specific assignment here on earth, this is called your purpose
2. Your purpose is the reason that you were born, it's the reason that you are on the earth today.
3. Your purpose assignment came/comes from God
4. God created the earth and all of its inhabitants for His plan, so your purpose is a part of His overall plan
5. You were given your assignment even before you were born
6. Your assignment is inter-related to the assignment of everyone else's within God's plan
7. Faith and commitment are the requirements for walking in your purpose and successfully completing your purpose.
8. Your Purpose is Your Superpower

EVERYONE HAS A PURPOSE

The very fact that everyone has a purpose should be acknowledged, accepted, and understood without fail. For obviously there is a reason that everyone is here on earth. But this statement needs to be taken even further because according to the Bible, everyone has a <u>Divine</u> Purpose! And I cannot over emphasize the word Divine in that statement.

After all, God first created man, and then He declared that He is the God of all flesh.[24] When God created man, He

---

[24] Jeremiah 32:27

created him as a 'living sou_'. Then He makes the declaration that all souls belong to Him.[25] David declared that we are all the children of the Most High.[26] God even says that He created us for His divine plan and pleasure (purpose).[27] So the Bible is explicit in declaring that everyone belongs to God, and hence, there is a divine reason that God placed us on this earth. But to understand that everyone has a Divine Purpose, you have to first understand God's plan for the world and the inhabitants that He created. This takes us all the way back to the creation of the first man Adam.

We know that all humanity was created by God to execute His plan on earth.[28] So effectively, in the first chapter of Genesis the earth and all humanity were created when God decided to expand His kingdom to earth.[29] His command to Adam and Eve were to go out, reproduce, and populate His kingdom.[30] (*Well, actually, the command was to re-populate the earth, but this a topic for another time*) At the end of the sixth day of creation, when Adam and Eve were the only two people in the Garden of Eden, God's kingdom on earth had been established and Adam and Eve had been given control over everything in the kingdom. Whatever God wanted done, Adam and Eve were there to do it. They were living in total bliss. Eden was God's Kingdom established on earth, and man was given the authority to

---

[25] Ezekiel 18:4
[26] Psalm 82.6
[27] Revelation 4:11
[28] Colossians 1:16; Ephesians 2:10; Ecclesiastes 12:13
[29] Genesis 1:26-31
[30] Genesis 1:28

rule over everything within this kingdom. Man reported up to God in this kingdom and only needed to be obedient to the God (the king) to remain forever in His newly established kingdom.

Then the influence of sin appeared, and it proved to be much stronger than the will of either Adam or Eve, so they succumbed to it. And this submission to the evil influence resulted in Adam and Eve being banished from Eden. But more importantly, and relevant to the topic of Divine Purpose, their banishment from Eden really meant that man had been removed from God's newly established kingdom. Access to Eden was now taken away from man, but his control on earth remained. Man remained on the earth, and in control, but without the bliss that he enjoyed when earth was the habitat of God's kingdom[31]. But God is faithful, so His plan to establish His kingdom on earth with man in authority remained. The Apostle Paul gives us an example of God's faithfulness, even in our failures, with his response to believers in Rome when they questioned why God still honored His assignment to Israel, even with all of their failures. The Apostle Paul stated that God will not change His mind (repent) on matters relative to His kingdom assignments.[32] And it is because God will not repent for His assignments, that Israel is still called and destined to be the priests for the earth. And so, being ever so faithful, even with the failure of Adam, God's plan to establish His kingdom on earth with man in authority remained; however, the implementation of His universal

---

[31] Genesis 3:17-24
[32] Romans 11:29

kingdom on earth would be paused until man returned to the state that Adam was in before he succumbed to the influence of sin. So the process of returning man back to the state that he was in, prior to the influence of sin, began.

As the population of the earth increased, God selected Abraham and instructed him that he would be the father of a nation of priests.[33] It is the function of a priest to connect and reconcile (reconnect) people with God. Therefore, this responsibility of reconciling humanity back to God became the Divine Assignment (purpose) of the descendants of Abraham (Israel). But Israel constantly and continually failed at this assignment. And with each failure the establishment of God's universal kingdom on earth was delayed. So God sent Jesus to do the work for which Israel had continually failed. But remaining ever so faithful, and while maintaining the integrity of the scriptures, God sent Jesus into this world through the descendants of Abraham; thereby keeping His priestly covenant with Abraham. Jesus could now reconcile man back to the state that man was in before Adam yielded to the influence of sin, and because Jesus was of Jewish ancestry, God's covenant with Abraham remained intact[34].

When the disciples asked Jesus to teach them to pray, Jesus said that they should pray that God's kingdom be established on earth like it is in Heaven.[35] But we know from reading the Apostle John's vision on the isle of Patmos that the universal establishment of God's kingdom

---

[33] Genesis chapter 17

[34] Hebrews 4:14-16

[35] Matthew 6:10

on earth won't occur until the seventh trumpet of Revelation.[36] Until that time, the kingdom of God is the state of submitting to God[37], and it is a personal decision that each and every individual has to make. But with the kingdom of God being inward and personal, and not the universal establishment that is God's plan, does not nullify God's plan to universally establish His kingdom on earth. That plan is still intact. But as stated earlier, the influence of sin caused a delay until man can be restored back to the state of man prior to the influence of sin. Until then, every person that is born on the earth is issued a Divine Assignment. It is divine because it is issued by God, and it is for the good of humanity. Your assignment on earth is issued to you to make your life, your community, your neighborhood, etc. better. It is your individual choice whether or not you will accept this assignment, or ignore it.

A huge misunderstanding comes when we associate Divine Assignment, or Divine Purpose, only with religion. Since God is the God of everyone, He makes assignments that are for the entire world, and many of the Divine Assignments, actually the overwhelming majority of them, are not religious or even connected to the church; else everyone born would be expected to have their primary role in religion or in the church. God wants us to be prosperous, successful, and victorious in every area of our lives, not just the area associated with the church or religion. So the overwhelming majority of people have been issued assignments that are not directly connected to the church,

---

[36] Revelation 11:15
[37] Luke 17:21; Romans 14:17

religion, or the temple. For these people, the church or the temple is yet very important, because God established this as the place for them to enter and worship, pray, praise, be encouraged, receive divine instruction, and be taught about God's desires for the present time. But after a worship session for the time is complete, these people were to return to their area of purpose and continue fulfilling their purpose until it was time to worship again. God's plan required that this process be continual and consistent, with the non-religious purposed people attending worship, and then returning to function in the area of their purpose. And the religious purposed people remaining at or around the temple, performing the work associated with the service of the temple. So when the religious purposed people needed food, they went to the people that were purposed to grow the food. When the religious purposed people needed clothing, they went to the people who were purposed to be seamstresses, tailors, shoemakers, etc. When the religious purposed people needed transportation, they went to the people who were purposed to build chariots, raise horses, etc. The plan is that everyone in their purpose would require the services of others who had purposes in other areas of life. In this everyone would be integrated into one harmonious humanity where everyone served a role that was vital to harmonious and successful living. This is God's plan as I will now show.

To show this, I will go to the numbers. Take a look at the picture below. I use this graphic in my purpose workshops.

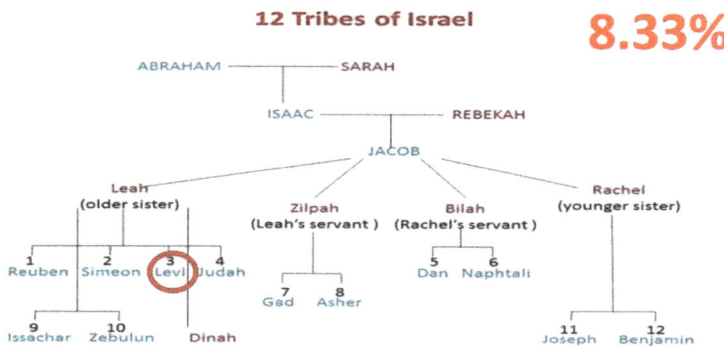

Shown are the twelve tribes of Israel that descended from Abraham, the same twelve tribes that God selected to be the priests for the world. We previously discussed that. But before they could become the priests to the world, they needed to be established as a nation. In their development into a nation, they needed to function in God's order. So God made His assignments to them. Of the twelve tribes, only one tribe was purposed to function as priests, meaning that this was the only tribe with Divine Assignments that were directly related to the functions of the temple, to religion functions, or to functions of the church. This meant that the tribe of Levi would serve as the preachers, the evangelists, the deacons, the choir, the ushers, the apostles, and all of the other religious vocations that were necessary to serve all of Israel. But one tribe out of twelve represents only 8.33% of the people. So God only gave religious purposes to roughly 8% of Israel. God created all of Israel for His plan, also, all of Israel were descendants of Abraham, therefore all of Israel had Divine Purposes; yet only 8.33% of those Divine Purposes were functions that were related to the temple, religion, or for us today, the church. So what of the remaining 11 tribes of Israel, or 91.66% (roughly 92%) of the people?

God is the holistic God of the entire world; therefore, His Divine Assignments represent the design of His plan to build up and support the entire world; to build up every man.[38] In God's kingdom on earth, all people are to function as servants to the king (God), just like the Angels do in God's kingdom in heaven. So the tribe of Levi's Divine Assignment within the nation of Israel was to provide the religious functions. The other tribes had capacities in which they served and fulfilled their Divine Assignments. God knew that people have to eat, so some people were given assignments (purposes) to farm, to raise livestock, or any of the other vocations related to creating the food that was to be eaten. God also knew that the people would need medical attention so some people were given assignments (purposes) as physicians, medical specialists, nurses, nutritionists, and all of the vocations related to medical care. God also knew that the people needed to pull back from their daily grind and relax, so some of the people were given assignments as entertainers, singers, performers, actors, actresses, and all of the vocations related to entertainment. Others were given assignments as teachers, athletes, engineers, administrators, politicians, reporters, etc. It was the assignment of the 8%

---

[38] Zechariah 14:9

of Israel who were purposed as the priests to provide religious services to the 92% of Israel that had assignments in other areas of life. This 8% also received the services of the 92% who were not purposed for religion. And likewise, the 92% of Israel that had assignments in the other areas of life provided their services to the priests, and the other tribes, while receiving services from those who were not purposed in their vocation. So the 92% came to the temple to worship, to hear from the Lord, to be exhorted, to be encouraged, and to be spiritually lifted; then they departed from the temple and went back to doing what God had purposed them to do. The tribe of Levi remained at the temple and functioned there because providing the religious functions and services was their assignment. And if everyone functioned accordingly in their assignments, as issued by God, then the twelve tribes of Israel would become a single nation, the nation of Israel; and the nation of Israel would exist in love, peace, and harmony while carrying out their national assignment within God's plan for the world. The entire process of the nation of Israel living in their Divine Purpose required an awesome implementation of reciprocity. An implementation with specific details and such crucial responsibilities that only a supernatural God could make it work and succeed. But that analysis is just with Israel, let's examine God's plan at the next level.

According to Worldometer, the nation of Israel represents less than 1% of the world's population[39]. And within God's

---

[39] Worldometer -- https://www.worldometers.info/world-population/israel-

plan for the world, Israel's assignment is to serve as the priests for the world.[40] Israel being less than 1% of the world's population means that more than 99% of the world is given assignments from God (purposes), that are not directly related to religion, the temple, or the church. This 99% represent the population of the world that have been given assignments to be the doctors, lawyers, athletes, entertainers, performers, engineers, teachers, politicians, counselors, etc. Simply put, in God's plan for the world, everyone has an assignment (purpose) given to them by God. God makes assignments to serve in every area of the world that's needed to support the holistic well-being of all of humanity.

So we see, first with Israel and then with the world, that within God's plan, everyone has a divinely issued purpose that holistically supports the entirety of humanity. And the majority of these assignments are **not** directly related to religion, the temple, the church, or any of the functions that are inherently directly connected to the temple, the church, or religion. And since it has been shown previously in this book that God is faithful and He does not change His plans regarding humanity, we can confidently declare that, even today, the majority of Divine Assignments are not directly related to religion, the temple, or the church. All Divine Assignments are related to the holistic well-being of everyone, and the improvement of the world for the entirety of humanity. AND GOD DOES NOT ESTEEMED ANYONE'S ASSIGNMENT TO BE BETTER OR MORE

---

[40] Exodus 19:6

IMPORTANT THAN ANYONE'S ELSE'S. Therefore, the challenge for everyone is to resist the influence of evil and prevent the perversion of your assignment. We should walk in our purpose ethically, morally, and with the highest level of integrity, while respecting the purposes of others. This should be done whether our assignments are directly connected to religion or not. As the Apostle Paul so eloquently exhorted us, we all should live a life that is worthy of the assignment for which we have been given[41] because the assignment has been given to us was given to make this world a better place for all humanity.

So your purpose, or your assignment, is indeed your SUPERPOWER! It is the area where you will experience unlimited success because it is the area that you were placed on this earth to function in. When living life in your purpose, you will shine! You will be the brightest star in the sky! You will be the most distinguished voice in the choral! You will be unbothered by external forces trying to make you fail! (*There are no failures when you are fulfilling your purpose, only lessons learned!*) Things will miraculously come together for you like never before! Your mistakes will become the building blocks that take you to even higher levels of success! There will be opposition, and I will devote an entire chapter of this book to overcoming opposition to your purpose; but when you are functioning within your area of purpose, you are simply unstoppable[42]! Opposition can't deter you, neither can it limit you or cause you to fail, because in this area, you are functioning with

---

[41] Ephesians 4:1
[42] Philippians 4:13

power; the power that works in you. And those that function in the area of their purpose always succeed[43]. But to better understand Divine Purpose, a working knowledge of predestination must be understood. Therefore, I have included a brief definition and functional example of predestination in the appendix.

[43] 2 Corinthians 2:14

The take-a-ways from this chapter that you need to retain as you read further in this book are:

1. Everyone has a purpose
2. Your purpose is divine because it was given to you by God, not because it is connected to the temple, the church, or religion
3. There are numerous areas for which people are purposed, and the majority of these areas are not directly connected to the temple, the church, or religion
4. God does not esteem one person's purpose higher than another's
5. You must fulfill your purpose morally, ethically, and with the highest level of integrity
6. You cannot fail if you function within the area for which God has purposed you
7. Again, your Purpose is Your Superpower!

DISCOVERING YOUR PURPOSE

As a pastor, one of the most frequently asked questions of me is, "Pastor, what does God want me to do?" or "Pastor, what am I here on earth to do?" What I'm really being asked is, "Pastor, can you tell me what my purpose is?" But identifying one's purpose is not something that another person can do for you, not even your pastor. Although I can coach, counsel, and provide direction to you on how to identify your purpose, the purpose identifying process always comes down to one person: YOU! This is because only two entities will actually know what your purpose is, God and you! God issued you the assignment so of course He knows, and He wants you to request this information from Him.

When I consider the ways that one identifies their Divine Assignment, a Shakespearean quote comes to mind.

> *"Be not afraid of greatness. Some are born great, some achieve greatness, and others have greatness thrust upon them."*
>
> **William Shakespeare**

This same statement can be said of discovering one's purpose. Mr. Shakespeare's statement could very easily be applied to purpose as "Some people's purpose is known at birth, some people acquire the knowledge of their purpose in the process of living, and yet others have their purpose thrust upon them." Note here that I am specifying how an individual acquires knowledge of their purpose. God knows your purpose because it was He who made the assignment. So it is without debate that the God of all of the earth, the God that knows the very number of hairs that crown your head, the God that has established Himself as the "Alpha and Omega, the Beginning and the End, the First and the Last," has knowledge of the assignment that He made to you; the work for which you were placed on earth to do. I have categorized the process of discovering your purpose into three methods. It has been my experience through the years, that everyone learns the reason why God placed them on earth by one of these three methods. I have found that the following three ways of discovering/identifying your purpose are:

1. For some, their purpose is identified at birth, or at a very early age,

2. For others, they learn of their purpose through the process of living life

3. Yet for others, the reason that God put them on earth will be thrust upon them at a time, such as in an emergency or other dire situation, when they are required to act or else

Either way, once your purpose is identified and once you begin fulfilling your assignment, immediate impact is experienced in the environment around you. The impact of you acquiring the knowledge of your purpose is remarkably profound. But before we expand on the three methods of purpose identification, let's make one major point that has to be understood:

WHEN YOU WERE BIRTHED INTO THIS WORLD, YOU WERE BIRTHED INTO THE ABSOLUTE BEST ENVIRONMENT FOR YOU TO SUCCEED IN YOUR PURPOSE!

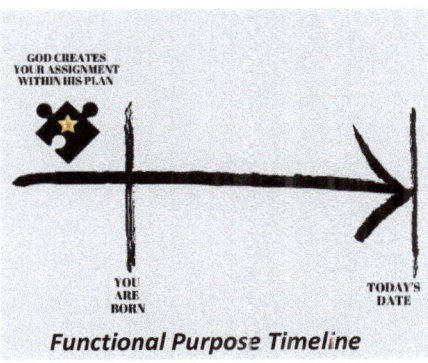

Functional Purpose Timeline

I created the timeline below and use it in an activity in my 'Discovering Your Life's Purpose' workshops.

What I am emphasizing with this timeline is that God has created your assignment within His plan before you were born. He knows what you must do in life, how you must do it, and the when(s) and where(s) of your life's events are scheduled within His plan. So with this foreknowledge, God positioned your entrance into the world under the very best conditions for you to succeed in your life's purpose. The Apostle Paul puts it this way in Romans chapter 8, verse 29:

> ***29. For whom he did foreknow, he also did predestinate to be conformed to the image of his Son, that he might be the firstborn among many brethren.***
> ***30. Moreover whom he did predestinate, them he also called: and whom he called, them he also justified: and whom he justified, them he also glorified.***

After reading the verses above, ask yourself this question based upon the very first phrase of Paul's statement in verse 29, **who did the omniscient God foreknow**? There can only be one answer to this question and that answer is **EVERYONE THAT HAS EVER BEEN BORN ON THIS EARTH**! (*Once again, I have included a functional definition of predestination in the appendix. Now may be a good time to review it.*) So since you were predestined at birth to arrive at an end result in which you are glorified, then you were positioned and set up at birth to succeed!

God's plan for you from your very beginning is that you experience the highest level of success in your life, and this high level of success occurs when you identify and walk in your purpose. And as I have previously shown, only a very small percentage of purposes are directly connected to the church, the temple, or religion. So God positioned you at birth to be successful as a doctor, a lawyer, an entertainer, a performer, a writer, a business executive, an athlete, a scientist, a dancer, a singer, a farmer, a restaurateur, etc. I think you get the point here. God positioned you to be successful while functioning in the area of your purpose, and your purpose supports humanity and the makes the world a better place. The entire world benefits when you function in the area for which God has purposed you. The timeline shown earlier will be re-visited because it is used in my purpose workshop to identify your purpose. In one activity, I have the participants create points on the timeline that represent major events, accomplishments, etc. You will see why this is a powerful activity in the next few pages of this book.

When you were born into this world, you were positioned for success in life. That's just how much God loves you! And being born positioned for success means that you were born at the exact right date and time for you to succeed in life; you were born in the right place for your success; you were born to the right parents for your success; the environment that you were born into was optimal for you to succeed. Everything about your entrance into this world, down to even the most smallest detail, was setup and positioned for you to experience success in your purpose. I often tell the participants in my workshops that even if your mother was a prostitute and your daddy was her pimp, God positioned you for success in your assignment within His plan. I know this can be a very difficult concept to grasp or to understand, but as we will see with the upcoming purpose discovery methods, God's plan for the world was created in inextricable detail. And in God's plan, the very smallest detail of your life has been deliberately planned to result in your success. Now back to the three methods of purpose identification.

Note that I am specifying a person acquiring knowledge of their purpose. It is without debate that the God of all of the earth, the God that knows the very number of hairs that crown our head, the God that is established as the "Alpha and Omega, the Beginning and the End, the First and the Last," the God who makes the purpose assignments to us, even before our arrival into this world, knows what He has assigned each of us to do within His plan, and within the world. But we must acquire this knowledge, and the following three ways are the ways that we do it.

Purpose Identified at Birth or at a very Early Age

This is probably the easiest and simplest way that a person's life's purpose is identified. God informs the parents prior to the birth, and they begin preparation for the child even before the child enters the world. This is possible because, as stated earlier in this book, every human is created as a living soul. And it is this soul that connects us to our creator. So God speaks to us with dreams, visions, or through urges, and unctions, etc. God knows us best and He definitely knows how to communicate His desires for us, to us. I've had numerous conversations with parents who have informed me how they've noticed "something different" about their child. So many times, they will inform me of the differences of their child compared to their other children, or to children in general. Some have stated that they had "a feeling" that their child would work in a certain profession, and the child ended up in that profession. Many times, this intuition does not occur at birth, but shortly thereafter, after they have had a few years observing the child.

This, I believe, is as God would have it be. God wants the parents, while functioning within their assignment, to counsel and guide their children into the assignment that He has for them. The family structure has been, is, and will always be foundational to God's plan for the world. This is why it so important to encourage and support your children when you notice that they are being creative or displaying an interest in positive things. Their youthful enthusiasm for a thing could be a revelation of the area of their purpose; the area in which they received their Divine Assignment.

And when we consider the typical life expectancy of man,[44] the sooner we identify and start fulfilling our purpose, the more time we get to enjoy our success and experience living life with our superpower! We have clear examples in the Bible of God informing the parents before birth, of their child's purpose in life, as well as examples of God informing the child at a very early age. Let's look at a brief example for each.

Samson – Purpose Identified Before Birth

In the thirteenth chapter of Judges in the Bible, we find that God sent an angel to the city of Zorah, to the wife of a man named Manoah. This angel had only one mission during this journey: to announce the forthcoming birth of Samson. But even greater than announcing the forthcoming birth of Samson, the angel also notified Manoah's wife of the assignment that God had given to her future son. The angel said to Manoah's wife before she was even pregnant with Samson, that her son was being put on earth to:

> *"be a Nazarite unto God from the womb:*
> *and he shall begin to deliver Israel out of the*
> *hand of the Philistines."*
> **Judges 13:5**

I like this because it validates a powerful point that was made earlier in this book. The Levites were the tribe that

---

had assignments from God that were directly related to the temple, the sanctuary, or religion within the nation of Israel. But the Bible specifically lets us know that Manoah was NOT of the tribe of Levi, but rather, he was of the Tribe of Dan[45]. We see in the lineage of Manoah, that God assigned Samson a purpose that was not connected to the functions of the Levites. Samson went to the temple to worship, to pray, etc., because this is the way God planned it; but his purpose was to be a great liberator, not a great priest. Samson's assignment was for the benefit of all of Israel. Those with religious purposes in Israel (the Levites) received the benefit of Samson fulfilling his purpose just as Samson received the benefit of those fulfilling their religious purposes. Is this not an example of God's Divine Assignments today? As previously stated, God's assignment to you, or to anyone else for that matter, is to improve our life, to improve your community, to improve the world. Samson's assignment from God was to be a soldier, a fighter for freedom, a liberator whose purpose would benefit the entire nation and make life better for everyone. Your purpose will always improve the harmonious living experience of humanity. It does this because your purpose is a piece of God's plan for the entire world.

Jeremiah – Purpose Identified at a Very Early Age

In the very first chapter of the biblical book of Jeremiah, we find a very young child named Jeremiah having deep conversations with His maker, who also happens to be the

---

[45] Judges 13:2

Purpose Giver. God informs Jeremiah of the reason that he was put on earth. God says to Jeremiah"

> *"Before I formed thee in the belly I knew thee; and before thou camest forth out of the womb I sanctified thee, and I ordained thee a prophet unto the nations."*
>
> **Jeremiah 1:5**

Regarding Jeremiah's age, the Bible only tells us that he was a young child[46]. I have seen scholars who have estimated his age to be as young as twelve years old, while other estimate his age to be in his early twenties. But the very young Jeremiah responded by using his youth as an excuse. God then supernaturally responded to Jeremiah's excuse. God's supernatural response convinced Jeremiah that his purpose was indeed his superpower! Jeremiah went on to do great things in his purpose, and both history and the Bible have recorded that his life exemplified the life of one upon whom God had smiled.

Because your purpose is your superpower, when you commit to fulfilling your purpose, God will step in and empower you to accomplish things that you could not otherwise accomplish. Your supernatural experiences will show you why the Apostle Paul declared that God always causes us to triumph[47]. God will never allow you to be

---

[46] Jeremiah 1:6
[47] 2 Corinthians 2:14

42

defeated or fail, your superpower empowers you to win! It empowers you to succeed! It empowers you to always be victorious!

Although identifying your purpose and walking in it at an early age is very desirable and definitely has its advantages, it is not the only way that purpose is identified; and relatively speaking, it is not the way that the majority of people will identify their purpose. Throughout my life as a believer, I have found this method to be the method that people credit the least as the method through which their purpose was identified.

Purpose Identified Through the Process of Living Life

The second method through which people identify their purpose is through the process of living life. As a pastor that has counseled numerous people that were distraught, exhausted, and frustrated, I've found that this is the method that most people have used to identify what their Divine Assignment is. Sometimes, I wish I had a quarter for every time I get asked, "Pastor, what did God put me here to do?", or "Pastor, what is my purpose?" Or for the many times that I hear the statement "Pastor, I don't know what I'm supposed to be doing." It's at these times that a little teaching, explanation, understanding, and life assessment is needed to provide the clarity and guidance necessary to identify your purpose. Using this method, I begin with a lesson on man's relationship with God.

First the teaching and explanation: We have already shown that God purposes each person before they are even birthed into this world; then, at birth, He places everyone on the path to fulfilling their purpose. This means, as stated earlier, that you were birthed into the world under optimal conditions to be successful in fulfilling your assignment. So if a person would just reject the influence of sin, then fulfilling your purpose would be a piece of cake. But the influence of sin is a powerful force. So powerful is this force, that without making a conscientious choice to seek help from God, it is impossible to overcome. Sin's influence is so powerful that the Apostle Paul declared that everyone has sinned.[48] So, prior to seeking help from God, we all succumb to the powerful influence of sin. Paul provides details of his struggle to overcome this influence without God.[49] He stated that, prior to seeking assistance from God, he often failed in his struggle to overcome the influence of sin; and furthermore, he stated that the very struggle itself left him broken and frustrated. Paul explained that he wanted to do good, but the influence of sin would overrule his desire to do good and he ended up doing evil. And this occurred frequently, continually, and with consistency. Paul teaches that the influence of sin will always overrule a person's desires to do good; so much so that he declared that in a person who has not sought help from God, the process of sin overruling the personal will to good is "a law". It's going to happen. But consider the state of Paul during his struggle to do good. Paul lets us know that he had not sought help from God. He was trying to overcome the influence of sin by himself. But even in that state, there was something within him that made him conscientious of right and wrong; and this something

---

[48] Romans 3:23
[49] Romans 7:15-24

within wanted him to do what was right, but it kept getting overruled by the influence of sin. And even though Paul consistently and continually yielded to the influence of sin, God did not destroy him, beat him up, or turn away from him; but rather God extended His arms of love and kept pulling at Paul to come to Him for help. In this we see the longsuffering of God towards Paul, and towards us[50]. God kept nudging Paul towards his purpose, even though Paul was in a stubborn state. This is how Paul ended up learning the law from the most acclaimed and highly esteemed scholar of his day. It wasn't that Paul was so righteous at the time, but because he was a living soul, <u>even in his stubborn and disobedient state, God orchestrated Paul's learning;</u> knowing that he would need this knowledge when he stepped up and started fulfilling his purpose.

God's longsuffering towards us is such that He doesn't cast us away in times of our stubbornness and disobedience, nor does He turn from us in the times prior to that point in our life that we come to Him, seeking His help to overcome the influence of sin. But as a loving father, He has patience and understanding; always accounting His plan for our desired end to be more important than our current failures. So instead of casting us away, He reaches for us and continually attempts to bring us to Him. And while He is attempting to bring us to Him, He is nudging us in directions that are necessary to acquire the things that we'll need at the time that we start fulfilling our purpose. This stubborn state is a state that every person born will eventually find themselves in. And until the time that we

---

[50] 2 Peter 3:9

45

accept the invitation from God requesting His help to overcome the influence of sin, Jesus intercede for us each and every time we fall short of God's desires for us.[51] So even though we were birthed into the world with an assignment in God's plan for the world, the influence of sin causes us to fail, until we seek help from God. This help comes through His son Jesus. But even in the times of our failure, God doesn't turn away from us, rather He displays longsuffering. It is in these times that being created as a living soul is most importance. The soul is the part of man that connects us to God.[52] It is with the soul that God uses to communicate with us, **even in our times of stubbornness and disobedience.** God may give us dreams, we may have intuitions, we may feel urges, we may experience unctions, we may be bothered by our conscience, etc. These all work to guide us to the best way, if we take heed and follow. Because God brought us here with an assignment, in the times prior to us having knowledge of Him, or seeking His help, He is longsuffering towards us; so instead of turning away from us, He keeps His extended hands reaching for us, all the time attempting to keep us on the path, or get us back on the path, to purpose fulfillment. Later in our lives, when looking back on these times, we realize that it was the hand of God directing us, and we didn't even know it. Have you ever done something and your conscience bothered you to the point that you had to undo it? That's God directing you via the soul. Have you ever had an unexplained urge to do something, and you did it, then later you learned of the

---

[51] 1 John 2:1
[52] Winning Spiritual Wars

catastrophe that would have occurred had you not done it? Once again, that's God directing you. Have you ever experienced an urge or an intuition, telling you to do something like take a class, get a certification, or learn a particular skill? Then later that class, certification, or skill was the reason that you received the job, or got the raise, or was able to achieve a certain thing? Again, I want you to know that these are all ways that God directs us, even in our disobedient times. God does all of this for us, and more, because He has placed us on a path to purpose fulfillment and success at birth; and He wants us to fulfill our purpose, experience success, and live our very best life. The understanding of how God relates to us is the centerpiece of this method of purpose discovery. So now, let's make some additions to the purpose timeline that we started earlier.

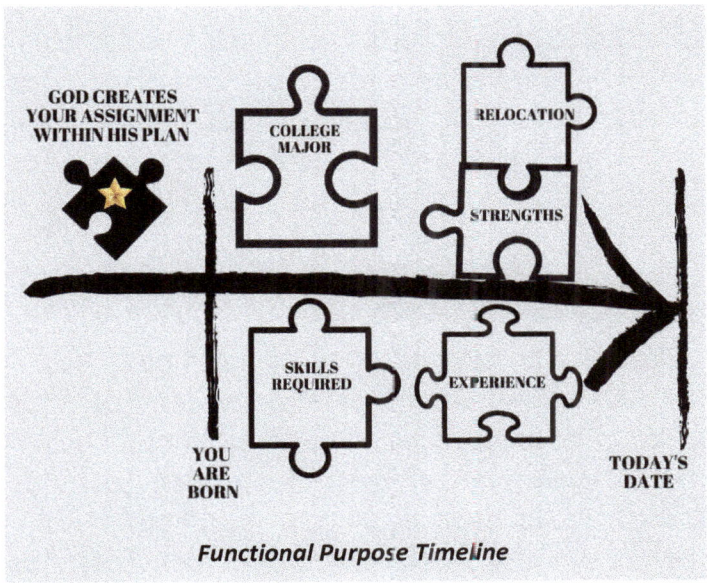

Functional Purpose Timeline

As you can see, we have added some points to our timeline. These points represent a few of the things that you may need to consider when trying to discover your purpose. What are your strengths? What do you do well with little or no effort? What are you educated or trained in? What skills do you have? Are any of your abilities rare or unique? What are the needs around you that you can supply? What is it that you do better than most but you do it without putting forth much effort? These are questions that you must ask yourself, and then provide honest and objective answers. The personal accomplishments and skills that you possess, you did not acquire them by coincidence. They are the result of you responding to the nudging of God via your soul, even when this nudging is unbeknownst to you. These accomplishments and skills were given to you, or you acquired them for a specific reason. You must realize and understand that you possess these things because of divine intervention; Intervention that occurred unbeknownst to you; Intervention that you cannot even begin to explain. This intervention occurred because you were created as a living soul, and every living soul that has ever populated this earth was placed here with a purpose.

(Keep in mind that God's plan is for the good of the world, and your purpose fits within His plan, therefore, your skills, education, knowledge, etc. come from Him and are to be used for good. This is a critically important point to understand because the primary goal of the influence of sin is to pervert your purpose for evil. The Influence of sin will take what was determined for good, and pervert it for evil. Many people, who are doing horrifically evil deeds, are using skills that were purposed

for good, but have been perverted for evil by the influence of sin.)

This timeline activity is a powerful tool to use if you are wondering just what God placed you on earth to do. You must be open and honest with yourself and be very objective when providing the answers to the various questions. And the questions that are listed above represent only a very small subset of the questions that must be asked. Many of your questions may be situational, personal, and/or specific; you may not have to ask yourself all of the available questions to arrive at your answer, but if you follow this activity through you will arrive at an assignment for which you are uniquely qualified. And this assignment, for which you are uniquely qualified, represents the reason that God placed you here on earth; to be specific, IT REPRESENTS YOUR PURPOSE!

Consider the life of the Apostle Paul. Paul's life is a perfect example of being directed by God; both before and after Paul sought God's help to overcome the influence of sin. Paul was born with freedom and the benefits of Roman citizenship[53], even though his people, the nation of Israel, were under Roman servitude. Paul was schooled and educated in the laws of Israel by the most highly esteemed scholar of his day[54]. Being born a Roman citizen, Paul was forced to acquire in-depth knowledge of both the Greek and Roman cultures. Many times, in scripture, Paul quoted the great Greek philosophers for which he possessed

---

[53] Acts 16:37; Acts 22:28
[54] Acts 22:3

comprehensive knowledge because of his studies.[55] All of these things just listed (*and there are more*) that Paul accomplished, happened before his encounter with God on Damascus Road, or they happened before what we commonly refer to as his Damascus Road Experience[56] . This means that Paul accomplished these things and acquired these skills and knowledge when he was in his period of stubbornness and disobedience; the time in his life before he sought God's help to overcome the influence of sin. Yet, it was these skills, accomplishments, and knowledge that served as the foundation of his work as the Apostle to the Gentiles. So we see that before his experience on Damascus Road, before he sought help from God to overcome the influence of sin, even in the time that he was committing evil against God, God did not turn away from him. But rather, God displayed longsuffering, because He knew what His assignment to Paul was. Therefore, He gently directed Paul's life before his conversion in ways so that when it was time for him to fulfill his purpose, he was equipped and ready. And this gentle directing of Paul was provided unbeknownst to Paul. In this we see the patience of God. Paul, being born at the right time, to the right parents, and in the right place, forced him to get the correct education and knowledge to successfully fulfill his purpose. It also provided him with a superb understanding of the Gentile cultures, and it gave him the appropriate freedoms that would be needed to fulfill his purpose.

---

[55] Acts 17:28; Titus 1:12
[56] Acts chapter 9

This happened to Paul before his conversion on the Damascus Road because he, like you and I, was birthed into this world and given an assignment, or purpose; and at birth he was placed on a path that was optimal for the successful completion of that assignment.

There are many things that are beyond our control, but since God is the one that makes the purpose assignments and controls the universe, He has accounted for those things from beforehand. He brought you into this world prepping you for your assignment and you didn't even realize it. So much of your past was really preparation for your purpose, and you won't realize it or understand it until such a time as you begin to walk in, and experience the successes of your purpose. At that time, you'll look back and say "now I see"! You've learned a lot, you've cried a lot, you've often been in pain, you've been beaten up a lot, etc. You didn't understand why these things were happening to you, or why this was your lot in life, then you realize that these things were the preparation for fulfilling your assignment, the preparation for walking in your purpose.

So many people that were born into poverty ended up finding their purpose in lifting others from poverty. Many that were born into broken families found their purpose in building strong families. Many that were birthed into violent and volatile environments find their purpose helping others achieve safety and peace. And through it all, they never realized that the afflictions, sufferings, and pains of their past were the preparation for walking in their purpose. When they realized this, they understood the miraculous divine interventions that allowed them to survive when other perished. The knowledge that God brought you along your path to prepare you for your assignment becomes obvious and apparent when you finally identify your purpose. You may have selected a career because you thought that it would lead to prosperity and great wealth, and it may very well do that, but when you become aligned with God you realize that your career path was planned by God beforehand, to prepare you for your assignment. You may have decided to relocate to a city because you fell in love with something, someplace, or someone that's located there. So you decided to relocate there and settle down, only to learn later that your relocation was a part of God's plan to bring you to your purpose.

You will find that your past experiences, your past pains, your past hurts, your accomplishments, etc., were all to prepare you for the assignment that God has issued to you.

But I am always asked, "Pastor, if I perform the timeline activity and identify an area and start working in what I believe to be my purpose, what will happen if it is really not my purpose? My response to this question is; after you honestly and objectively do the timeline activity, just start working. And if this is not your purpose area, then surely God will re-direct you to your purpose area because, just by getting started on what you think is your purpose, you are showing a sincere desire to do what He has placed you here to do. God always responds to sincere desires. We see an example of God re-directing Paul in Acts 16:6

"Now when they had gone throughout Phrygia and the region of Galatia, and were forbidden of the Holy Ghost to preach the word in Asia"

Paul knew that he had a purpose, and his purpose was to preach to the Gentiles. But when he was heading to Asia to preach, God forbade him to go, but rather pulled him back and re-directed him another way. So just as God re-directed Paul, He can and will re-direct you, if necessary. If you just get started using your achievements, expertise, knowledge, skills, etc., for good and positive impact, if God wants you to do another thing or go another way, He has shown that He has the ability to direct you as He will. Even though I get asked this question quite frequently, after performing the timeline activity with the following five step process, most people experience results that gives them confidence and satisfaction that they are now on their way to fulfilling their purpose.

Here is the five-step process that I recommend for utilization of this method to identify your purpose.

1. Align yourself with God. This is a requirement so that you discover and understand who you are in God. You can do this by actively reading the Bible and commit to consistent prayer. The Bible is filled with verses on who God is, and who He says you are. You will discover that God created you with a unique and valuable purpose. By understanding who you are, you will be empowered to live the greater life that He desires for you. We were never meant to do life alone so we could all use

help along the way. Prayer and reading the Bible is that help. You don't have to pray and read for long periods of time if you are not currently doing either. I usually recommend that people start their day with a short prayer, and a verse. This may take five minutes or less, but these minutes will become a very powerful five minutes. If you can pray and read longer, then of course that is something that I recommend. And if you are concerned that you are not living in alignment with God, this short prayer is a great time to just ask for clarity, guidance, and assistance. God will answer you and remind you of the assignment that He has issued to you. He will then give you strength, wisdom and confidence to live in alignment.

2. Perform a thorough, comprehensive, honest, and objective life audit. In this audit, you identify, analyze, and note any major things that have taken, or are currently taking up time, space, mental energy, and physical energy in your life. With this you want to comprehensively and thoroughly look back over the details of your life from birth to date, as best as you can remember. I have found that the impactful things are forever etched in memory. Note the environment in which God placed you at birth, the people that influenced you, the obstacles that you have overcome and the lesson learned while overcoming; list the victories, the high points, and the low points, etc. The goal is to identify the people, situations, events, etc. that God

used to bring you through your hardships, the things that He used to develop you, and bring you to where you are today.

3. Perform a comprehensive personal skill assessment. Your skills describe what you are good at. You develop skills by working, through training and by becoming experienced in an area; and these skills improve your ability to do tasks. *Remember, your acquisition of these beneficial things didn't happen by coincidence, but they were divinely orchestrated.* Being able to identify and describe your skills allows you to answer the key questions about yourself such as: *What is it that I do really well? What problems can I solve? Where are my strengths?*

4. Seek God for guidance and the positive opportunities in which to use your skills, your expertise, your strengths, your knowledge, etc. God wants to provide the guidance that you are in need of[57]. But so many times we simply fail to seek Him for this advice and counsel. We try to do it all by ourselves.

5. Start using your skills, your experience, your knowledge, your strengths, etc., for positive activities. **When you know what you bring to the table, start bringing it. Don't wait to be asked or invited, volunteer!**

So if you are yet wondering what your purpose in life is, or why God has placed you on earth, this method is

---

[57] Isaiah 58:11

specifically for you. Take the time to perform both the timeline activity and, and the five-step self-examining audit. I am sure that you will come away enlightened as to what your purpose really is.

Purpose Thrust Upon You

It has been said that you never know how strong you are until strength is your only choice for advancement or survival.

Singer Bernice Johnson Reagon put it this way, *"**Life's challenges are not supposed to paralyze you; they're supposed to help you discover who you are.**"* And with this powerful quote I begin explaining the third method for identifying your life's purpose: Having your purpose thrust upon you.

The challenges we face in life will become extreme at times, forcing us into states of mental anguish that are exhausting for even the strongest of personalities. But it is these challenges that are often used to force you into your purpose. With this method of purpose discovery, an extreme challenge presented becomes an enormous opportunity to step up and do what you were put here to do.

I have previously shown that in the course of life, through divine intervention, we acquire skills, experience, knowledge, etc., that serve as the preparation for us stepping up and doing what God placed us on earth to do. But even then, stepping up and moving out into our area of purpose can be a daunting task. It's taking a lot of audacity, boldness, confidence, courage, nerve, and plain old grit to make that move. So sometimes, when God sees that you are ready, but still not moving out into your purpose, He will configure the environment around you in such a way that you are forced to act or else. He will place you in situations where a particular skill or certain knowledge is the only thing that can successfully bring you through. And when you look for others to possess that needed skill or knowledge and take the lead to do what needs to be done, you discover that there is no one available but you. And after all of your anxiety, tears, feeling sorry for yourself, complaining, begging, etc. that you do, still no one appears to do what needs to be done, so you are forced to step up and do it. You are forced to take inventory within, become creative, and employ self-motivation to make happen what you know needs to happen. And when you step up, you realize that you possess exactly what is required to make it happen. You met the requirements all along. God had been preparing you for this since birth, so this challenge only served to awaken you to that purpose! You already possessed the knowledge. You already possessed the skills. You'd been concealing your creativity. You have the will. You have the energy. And the fear of what will happen if you don't act provides you with the necessary motivation! CONGRATULATIONS! You have just had your purpose thrust upon you! Surely you were placed on this earth for a time such as this.

It reminds me of a story that I once heard. The story goes like this: There were four friends named, Somebody, Anybody, Everybody, and Nobody. They were all at work one day and a very important task popped up that had to be done. It was an urgent task that required immediate attention. Somebody looked at the task and said, "Oh, this is an easy task, anybody can do this", then he walked away. Soon thereafter, anybody walked up. He too looked at the task but said, "Why should I do this when everybody should have to do it". He too, walked away. A little later Everybody came upon the task. He mumbled to himself "I know the others saw that this needs to be done. I'm always stuck bailing them out, but not this time." And Everybody, just like Somebody and Anybody before him, walked away and left the task undone. So guess who was left to do the task; that's right, NOBODY! When your purpose is thrust upon you, you can look for Somebody, Anybody, or Everybody to step up, take the lead, and do the work; but the reality is that Nobody will be only one who will address your need, the only one that you can count on; so in the end, if you want to get it done, you will have to step up and do it yourself! I could tell you the biblical story of Moses, who had his purpose thrust upon him when God determined that it was time for Israel to leave Egypt. I could also acquaint you with the story of Queen Esther, who was forced into her purpose when her people faced extinction because of jealousy and prejudice. The Bible is full of stories of people that had their purpose thrust upon them. But there are even more compelling and relative current examples of one's purpose being thrust upon them, and I'm sure you are aware of at least one such incident.

In late 2019, people begin to fall ill with a mysterious illness. The progression of this illness was fast and the results of being infected were fatal to many. It was named the Coronavirus, and by March of 2020, the impact of this virus was such that the World Health Organization declared it to be a global pandemic. With no known cure, uninhibited spread, and rising fatalities, the Coronavirus pandemic forced the world to basically shut down. We were told to quarantine in our houses. Offices shut down. Businesses had to close. Travel ceased. Houses of Worship were shuttered. Only those deemed to be 'essential workers' were allowed to work. Yet, the rent still had to be paid. Food still had to be purchased. Education needed to continue. Although we were in a pandemic, there was still needs that had to be supplied if we were to continue living. This is when millions of people discovered their Divine Purposes! They started looking within themselves and becoming creative. They started using their skills, education, knowledge, training, etc. to provide life sustaining income. They opened businesses that were suited for the pandemic environment. Some started baking and selling their product. Some started designing clothing and marketing their product. Some started marketing the businesses of others. Numerous businesses were created, and numerous people were catapulted into their area of purpose because of the pandemic. Simply put, in the midst of a global pandemic, they had their purposes thrust upon them. They realized that they possessed within themselves the tools necessary to survive; and not only to survive, but to thrive, progress, and reach levels of success that they hadn't even *asked for or thought of.*[58] They realized that they had been prepared for a time such as this, even though their preparation occurred unbeknownst to them. And they became successful in their endeavors, and they continue to

---

[58] Ephesians 3:20

succeed. So great is their success that when the pandemic waned, many refused to return to their previous places of employment, choosing to continue in their newly created occupation. And with this they have created for themselves businesses and careers where they are the CEO, and their continued success depends entirely upon them.

The publisher that publishes my books is one of those entrepreneurs. She often tells of how the office where she worked was closed because of the pandemic, so she decided to write a book. Then upon writing it and going through the publishing, marketing, and release process to get her book to the public, she had an urging, or unction, or a leading to start a publishing company and provide this service to other authors who wished to share their stories with the world. I consider her story to be validation for divine intervention because of the way I gained knowledge of her company. It was a miraculous connection that resulted in my first book with her company becoming a Best-Selling New Release. Today she has authors lining up for her services, and her company is no longer a one-person business. She has employed others because of business expansion. It is inspiring, encouraging, and motivational just hearing her tell of her publishing company's journey, a journey that commenced in the midst of a global pandemic.

So there you have it; the three methods through which purpose is identified. And once you identify your purpose, you need to commit to fulfilling it and experiencing the success that functioning in your SUPERPOWER brings.

The take-a-ways from this chapter that you need to retain as you read further in this book are:

1. There are three ways through which purpose is Identified
2. Use of the purpose timeline activity to arrive at your purpose
3. Use the five-step process for using life experiences and past accomplishments and progress to identify your purpose
4. God has a vested interest in your purpose, so He communicates with you, even in times of stubbornness and disobedience, to ensure that you have ample opportunity to fulfill your purpose
5. Your soul is your connection to God in the spirit realm, and it is through this that God will give us urges, unctions, intuitions, etc. for direction
6. Your past experiences, achievements, accomplishments, skills acquired, knowledge acquired, etc. we're preparing you for your Divine Purpose.

DEFEATING THE ENEMIES OF YOUR PURPOSE

It has been put forth as a wise saying that "the enemy of my enemy is my friend". I don't agree with this statement, for a variety of reasons, nor do I agree with the paradigm that it conveys. But using a similar paradigm, one might say with truth that "the enemy of my friend is also my enemy." In other words, you will acquire enemies, not because of something that you did to them, nor will the reason be because of something that you said about them, neither is it because they hold positions that are directly or indirectly in opposition to your positions; but you will acquire enemies simply because they are the enemies of your friends.

I opened with that paradigm because when considering opposition to your purpose, the enemies that you will encounter, the forces that are trying to stop you, and the opposition that's fervently working to bring about failure in your life, are first and foremost the enemies of God. They are established in opposition to God's plan for humanity. They have stepped up and committed to work for the failure of God's plan; and since your assignment is a part of God's overall plan for the world, they are working to force failure upon you as well. These enemies would like to force failure on everyone in God's plan that has assignments, or purposes. And since God's plan includes every living person, THIS MEANS THAT THEY ARE OPPOSING YOU! The enemies of God's plan become the enemies of your purpose because your purpose is but a part of God's plan. It may appear that the easiest solution for you is to not commit to your purpose, but with non-committal, you forfeit the successes and victories that come with functioning within your superpower; and that forfeiture results in a life of anguish, distress, despair, stress, and hopelessness. So since you are already on this earth, you might as well get every benefit, claim every victory, rise to your highest height, and live your very best life. And to do this you must be driven to complete your Divine Assignment; you must or fulfill your purpose regardless of the forces that oppose you. You must commit to win. And why not? You can't lose when you commit to fulfilling your purpose because you are empowered by the supernatural purpose giver; He's assisting you and assuring you of victory. It's like you are in a fixed fight that you can't lose, as long as you stay focused on what you have been assigned to do.

But even with your victory assured, you will encounter opposition, so you must prepare yourself.[59] And with every weapon that is used against you by the opposition, you must be confident that you are predestined to win, so those weapons will fail.[60] And every plot that is devised against you will come to naught. The purpose giver will make all of the bad plans that the opposition enacted against you, work for your good.[61] So instead of failures, the attacks will become lessons learned, steps to your higher ground, and building blocks for your success.

In this chapter we will examine some of the common enemies of your purpose and explain how to confront and defeat them when they appear. This is by no means an attempt to cover every weapon that the enemies of your purpose will use, because they are too numerous. But the strategies used to put down the common and frequently encountered enemies can successfully be applied in other areas as needed. So let's take on the enemies of your purpose.

---

[59] 1 Peter 4:1
[60] Isaiah 54:17
[61] Romans 8:28

FEAR

To be afraid of (someone or something)
as likely to be dangerous, painful, or
threatening.

The first enemy of your purpose that must be addressed is fear. I begin with fear for some very obvious reasons; reasons for which you will understand shortly. Of all of the weapons that oppose your purpose, fear is one of the most effective, if not the most effective, weapon of opposition that you will encounter. Fear is so powerful because it performs two impactful functions:

1. Fear freezes you in place. It freezes you in a state of despair, perplexity, hopelessness, etc. And since you haven't begun living your life in your purpose area, you haven't experienced the results of your superpower at work. So effectively, fear freezes you in failure

2. Fear prevents you from even getting started with life in the area of your purpose area. The enemies of your purpose are not very smart, but even they understand that preventing you from getting started is the most effective way to ensure that you will not finish.

You must understand that the forces that oppose your assignment know all too well that your purpose is your superpower. And these forces will work extremely hard to keep you separated from that power. The most effective strategy of any army is to cut off the opposition's access to their power source. When countries wage war against each other, some of the very first targets that they attempt to eliminate are the power sources of their enemies. They do this first because they understand that without power, their enemy becomes immobile; essentially, their enemy becomes frozen in place, and severely weakened. It takes power to accomplish anything, especially to wage war. Fear has proven to be a very effective weapon because it essentially keeps you separated from your inherent superpower, the superpower that you become once you live life in the area of your purpose. God's purpose for you makes you ever so powerful, but if you allow fear to keep you from your area of purpose, then all of that power lies dormant within you. Fear prevents you from using the *"power that works in you*[62]*."* You become as one that possesses a weapon, but lacks the strength to use it. You must defeat fear!

Relative to purpose, fear most often presents itself as a fear of failure. If we don't understand the power that's invested in us, fear tells us that we will fail because we lack the ability to do all that is necessary for success. Fear will convince you that you are inadequate, unprepared, unqualified, or simply just not enough to do what God has placed you here to do. This naturally leads to a fear of failing in your assignment. And if you believe that failure will ultimately be the outcome, then why even expend the energy necessary to get started? But you must stand up to fear, being convinced that you do possess the ability

---

[62] Ephesians 3:20

because you have been empowered.[63] You must be convinced within yourself that you are not standing alone, that there is power within you,[64] and this power has been given to you by the purpose giver.

I will take just a brief moment and reference Ephesians 3:20. In this verse the Apostle Paul teaches:

> *"Now unto him that is able to do exceeding abundantly above all that we ask or think, according to the power that worketh in us"*

When I was growing up, this verse was continually and consistently used to teach that the Holy Spirit empowers us when we receive it. And it is true that the Holy Spirit does empower us, but according to the Bible, the Holy Spirit empowers us with the power that we need to be effective witnesses for the Lord,[65] and this power to witness effectively can take on many functions, forms, roles, and responsibilities, but ultimately, the objective of this power is to make us effective witnesses for Christ. But *"the power that worketh in us"* that Paul is talking about in Ephesians chapter 3, verse 20, is the power that we possess when we live in the area of our purpose. It is the power of a faithful and loyal 'living soul', living a life that's committed to the purpose giver. It is the power of a life committed to the one who has issued all of our Divine Assignments. Simply put, *"the power that worketh in us"* is the power that we

---

[63] Philippians 4:13
[64] Ephesians 3:20
[65] Acts 1:8

possess when we are completing our purpose; IT'S OUR SUPERPOWER!

When dealing with fear, you must keep three things in mind.

1. Fear **NEVER** comes from God! **2 Timothy chapter 1, verse 7**, explicitly states that "***God has not given us the spirit of fear***"! So regardless of the place in your life that you experience fear, just know that it is not from your purpose giver, so it must be resisted and rejected.

2. God does not call the qualified; He qualifies those whom He calls. Consider Jeremiah.[66] I love this and I believe that you will love it too. When God is informing Jeremiah of his purpose, Jeremiah responds that he is unqualified because of his youth. God immediately qualifies him, and with his newly acquired qualifications, Jeremiah starts fulfilling his purpose. Now think back to the purpose discovery methods that were presented earlier in this book, God has used your past experiences, accomplishments, achievements, etc., to also qualify you for your assignment. Now, the world awaits the beginning of your work.

3. Your purpose is an assignment from God. If God makes the assignment, He then is responsible for empowering you to succeed. You only need to trust the process. When you are living life within your area of purpose, you are empowered to accomplish,

---

[66] Jeremiah chapter 1

achieve, succeed, overcome, and be victorious. Have confidence in the purpose giver. Confidence in the purpose giver's overall plan will create confidence in your part of the plan. And confidence in your part of the plan motivates you to overcome any obstacles to fulfill your purpose. Always keep in mind the purpose giver's track record; HE NEVER FAILS.[67]

There is really only one way to overtake fear and prevent it from keeping you away from your purpose.

YOU MUST CONFRONT FEAR IN FAITH!

You must have faith in the purpose giver, His plan, and His assignment to you within His plan. The writer of Hebrews tells us that:

> *"But without faith it is impossible to please him:* "
> **Hebrews 11:6**

You please the purpose giver by fulfilling your assignment; by walking in your purpose. And you cannot do this without having faith in the one that issued you the assignment! This is how Peter overcame his fear when he

---

[67] Joshua 21:45

walked on water with Jesus[68]. Know that fear won't disappear without a fight. It will fight back with fervor. It will present destruction as your end result. And with every bump in the road, fear will show you failure. You will be inundated with examples of others failing. Even after you muster up enough courage to confront your fear and start fulfilling your purpose, fear will keep showing you failure. But the more you work in your purpose area, the more your confidence will build. And the more your confidence builds, the more you are motivated to keep going. And the more motivation that you have, the greater your expectations for success will become. And the greater your expectations for success becomes, the more work you will do. It's a process,[69] and the process will keep repeating itself until your success becomes a way of life. The booklet, '*The 4 Principles of Dominion Authority*', teaches how to make success a repeatable process, thereby making it a lifestyle. Every day that you continue, after confronting your fear, increases your faith. And every increase in your faith emboldens you to continue with even more fervor, more authority, more confidence, more commitment, and with the anticipation of more success. But this all begins with confronting your fear in faith.

When you confront your fear in faith, the results will be so profound, and your life will elevate in such a way, that you will have to proclaim just as the Apostle Paul did:

---

[68] Matthew 14:24-31
[69] Romans 5:3-5

> *"Now thanks be unto God, which always causeth us to triumph in Christ"*
>
> **2 Corinthians 2:14**

When you start confronting your fear to fulfill your purpose, you are on your way to constant and continual victory, you will always triumph!

Depression

more than just sadness, depression is a common and serious medical illness that negatively affects how you feel, the way you think and how you act. According to Access Community Health Network, depression is classified as a mental illness

As fervent a fight as fear confronts you with to keep you from getting started with your purpose, depression matches or exceeds that fervency in an attempt to force you to quit living your purpose after you've started. Relative to your purpose, depression is a formidable enemy that has but one mission to accomplish: it comes to force you to cease functioning in your purpose. The intensity of a depression attack can range from a minor emotional feeling, all the way up to a crippling mental state; a mental state that could lead to self-harm or even death, if not properly addressed. When depression confronts you, it is on a mission to force you to quit, or to eliminate you all together. This is an enemy that you just can't ignore, you must know how to put this enemy down, and keep it down. Using a common board game analogy, depression is playing chess, so if you are prepared for checkers, you are in big trouble.

The reason that depression is such a formidable enemy is that it is a spiritual ailment that manifests itself in the natural world. Remember, that all humans are comprised of body, soul, and spirit.[70] (*For a detailed and comprehensive explanation of the make-up of man, pick up a copy of*

---

[70] 1 Thessalonians 5:23

Winning Spiritual Wars- Unleashing the Power of the Soul.)

The Constitution of Man

The very way that we are created gives enemies that reside in the spiritual world the ability to attack and have impact in the natural world. And this is just what depression does.

The understanding of the construction of man is necessary when confronting depression. This knowledge is comprehensively explained in the book, ***Winning Spiritual Wars, Unleashing the Power of the Soul***, so I will build upon that knowledge foundation.

All humans possess dual citizenship. Being created as living souls, we have residency in both the natural world, and the spiritual world. Your physical body is you in the natural world, whereas your soul is you in the spiritual world. It is the spirit that made man a 'living soul',[71] it is also the spirit that 'quickens'[72] our mortal (physical) bodies. This makes your body 'natural', and your soul 'supernatural'. (*All created beings that reside in the spiritual world are not constrained by natural limitations, hence they are supernatural.*) So we have residency in both the natural and spiritual worlds. The **mind** is a part of the soul. The mind also possesses dual consciousness. It has consciousness in the natural world via the body, and as a part of the soul, it inherently possesses consciousness in the supernatural world. The mind of man represents *the presence of the supernatural soul in the natural world*.[73] As such, the mind provides the powers, spirits, and beings that reside in the spiritual world with access to the natural world. In plain terms, it provides natural access to the supernatural. This is the power of the mind.

This access, however, was only intended to be utilized by the soul, or the part of us that inherently makes us God's children. But knowing the dual consciousness of the mind, and that he can impact the natural world through it, Satan and his evil angels are constantly waging war to gain control of your mind, and if not complete control, they will settle for access and residency in your mind. That brings us to depression.

As stated earlier, depression is a spiritual ailment that manifests itself in the physical, or natural. As a spiritual

---

[71] Genesis 2:7
[72] Romans 8:11
[73] Winning Spiritual Wars pp 39-53

ailment, it needs access to the natural to be effective. It gets this access by taking up residency in the mind. Hence, it is medically classified as a **mental ailment**.

When depression sets up in your mind, it begins to impact your physical body, character, and environment, even when you don't have any medically diagnosed or actual physical ailments. This validates the power that the mind can have on the physical body! You begin to feel bad because depression says that you feel bad. I've known people who were battling depression that were convinced that they were medically afflicted, but after numerous doctors' visits, and countless diagnostic scans and tests revealed no physical medical ailment, their depression was diagnosed. Depression will tell you that you are the only one dealing with a certain issue; and the impact of this is that you will begin separating and withdrawing yourself from others, withdrawing to a lonely place. Depression will make you feel sad even when your environment is gleeful and you are experiencing no natural negative occurrences in your life. Depression is such a powerful force that it has caused people to harm others, even harm themselves. The ultimate goal of depression, relative to your purpose, is to force you to cease functioning in the area of your purpose, but its end game is to eliminate you. This enemy knows that if you are taken out altogether, the opportunity to reset and restart fulfilling your purpose no longer exists, with you being absent from the world. Consider the impact that depression had on the prophet Elijah.

In 1 Kings Chapter 19, we find the prophet Elijah struggling with depression immediately after a period in which he experienced the miraculous power of God. He had been on Mount Carmel where he had just experienced God send fire from Heaven in the presence of over 850 false prophets, and a crowd of people. And this display of God's power was directly in response to his request. So his superpower was at work. Surely such an awesome display of God's power should be encouraging, motivating, and exhilarating. But instead of celebrating and rejoicing, he found himself in the crosshairs of an angry queen; a queen who'd been embarrassed and suffered defeat at the display of God's power. So he ran away from everyone (separated to a place alone). *Remember that one of the tactics of depression is to separate you from others and get you alone.* And from his lonely place he complained to God. This is what he said:

> *"But he himself went a day's journey into the wilderness, and came and sat down under a juniper tree: and he requested for himself that he might die; and said, It is enough; now, O LORD, take away my life; for I am not better than my fathers."*
> **1 Kings 19:4**

IS THIS NOT DEPRESSION IN ITS MOST POWERFUL FORM? Remember that depression wants to eliminate you, or take you out of this world, to ensure that you don't fulfill your purpose. So instead of rejoicing, Elijah is alone, sad, and saying that he would be better off dead. By Elijah complaining and requesting to die, we see exactly where depression was trying to take Elijah. Elijah wasn't the only one.[74] But if depression is successful in getting you to a dark lonely place, it will speak lies to you, with the goal of taking you out altogether. Whenever I read this, I thank God that Elijah knew enough, even in his dark place, to talk things over with the purpose giver. And if you find yourself falling into a dark place, have confidence that God will be there for you, just like He was there for Elijah. In recent times, the church has been maligned by many who have had bad experiences within the church, or have had bad interactions with people in leadership within the church. But God's true church is comprised of people who sincerely work to improve the lives of others, and are committed to serving humanity. It is their purpose. And if you ever find yourself in a dark place during turbulent times, a church of true believers could be your life saver.

Depression doesn't necessarily attack alone. Frequently it is in collusion with anxiety. These two enemies of your purpose team together so frequently, that the Mayo clinic states:

> *"Anxiety may occur as a symptom of clinical (major) depression. It's also common to have depression that's triggered by an anxiety disorder, such as generalized anxiety disorder, panic disorder or separation anxiety disorder. Many people have a diagnosis of both an anxiety disorder and clinical depression."*[75]

---

[74] Romans 11:1-4
[75] Mayo Clinic

Anxiety is defined as *"is a feeling of fear, dread, and uneasiness. It might cause you to sweat, feel restless and tense, and have a rapid heartbeat. It can be a normal reaction to stress"*[76] It's relatively easy to see the connection between depression and anxiety. It's also easy to understand how anxiety can serve as a trigger for depression. The stress of anxiety can impact your physical body with conditions such as high blood pressure; and conditions like high blood pressure can have debilitating physical effects on your body. But the instructions that we are given concerning anxiety is:

"Be careful for nothing; but in every thing by prayer and supplication with thanksgiving let your requests be made known unto God."
Philippians 4:6

Throughout this book, I've been using the King James Version of the Bible for my biblical references, so I continued using it here for consistency. But more recent translations provide clarity to this verse by translating the first phrase of that verse as *"**Be anxious for nothing**."* This difference in reading reflects the improved knowledge and understanding of the historical biblical languages that scholars today possess. The original text, in the original language, remains; however, knowledge and understanding

---

[76] MedlinePlus(gov) --

of the historical language has improved tremendously since the King James translators did their work.

So we are instructed to let nothing make us anxious. Having confidence in the purpose giver allows us to live with such level of confidence. And if we allow nothing to make us anxious, then anxiety can't become the trigger for depression. Depression, itself, is a powerful enemy to your purpose. It is formidable when attacking alone, but anxiety creates another level for which you must consider in the fight. But as formidable and powerful of enemy that depression can be, we have been empowered and equipped for our purpose, therefore we have been empowered to overcome it, defeat it, and put it down.

Before I begin explaining how we must confront and defeat the enemy of depression, it is imperative that I make the following statement of fact regarding your response when confronting this enemy. As a pastor that is followed by many, I know that there are those that listen to my teachings and apply them. This statement is especially for them.

As a pastor, I would never recommend or suggest that anyone ever forgo proper medical treatment for any ailment that afflicts them. This remains true for the ailment of depression. There are trained medical professionals who specialize in treating this ailment; I recommend that their assistance be sought when confronting depression. Depression, however, is a complicated mental ailment that has spiritual origins, but impacts the natural, or the physical. Therefore, I

always recommend that this ailment be addressed both medically, and spiritually, to ensure complete elimination, and to guard against future attacks.

That being said, let's look at what we must do, in addition to medical treatment, to aggressively confront depression and put it down, defeat it, or overcome it. To overtake depression, we need to first know *__who we are and what God has placed in us as living souls__*. There was a time when Israel was aimlessly toiling, but not fulfilling their purpose. God had provided the tools that they needed to successfully complete their assignment, but instead of learning about and applying the tools, they continued aimlessly toiling and continually failing. Even though the solution of their problems existed and was available, they simply didn't put in the effort or take the time to learn this solution and apply. So God said of them while they were in this state:

> *"My people are destroyed for lack of knowledge: because thou hast rejected knowledge"*
> **Hosea 4:6**

When you have the knowledge of who you are and the power that God has invested in you as a living soul, you can then use what God has put in you to put down this powerful enemy, before it puts us down. That's right; depression is an enemy that attempts to prevent you from ever walking in your purpose by putting you down. Its goal is to deceptively trick you into ending it all. THIS IS WHY SO MANY TIMES, UNTREATED DEPRESSION LEADS TO SUICIDE. But when equipped with the knowledge that there is power that works within you; power that, once you align with God, becomes activated and empowers you to great things, you can defeat this enemy. This is the power to do even more that you can ask or think. And this power works in you! Commitment to fulfill your purpose activates this power, and depression must submit to you when you are in fulfilling your purpose. The Apostle Paul put it this way when giving honor to the purpose giver:

> *"Now unto him that is able to do exceeding*
> *abundantly above all that we ask or think,*
> *according to the power that worketh in us"*
> **Ephesians 3:20**

So knowledge and understanding are principal assets for you when confronting depression. When you are aware of the power that you possess, it sets your expectation to victory. When you understand that this enemy is spiritual, you know that in addition to proper medical treatment, you must also confront it spiritually. Speaking of medical treatment for depression, I must tell this short story because I accepted it as divine confirmation for this portion of this book. I've been writing this book for quite a while, using prayer, Bible study, and research as I write. I had been writing for over three hours one day and just as I got to this section on depression, I took a break to get away from my computer for a while. I got up, left my basement office, and went upstairs, hoping to sit and talk with my wife for a while before retiring for the night. Just as I entered the room where she was watching television, a commercial came on, and like a magnet, I was drawn to the TV. It was a commercial for an anti-depressant. The narrator went through the benefits of this particular anti-depressant, but the emphasis was that it was 65% more effective in relieving the symptoms of depression than comparative medications. The narrator made that statement with emphasis, then, as if a light shined brightly within me, it hit me why depression must be confronted spiritually in addition to medical treatment. The treatment that the narrator of that commercial spoke of was successful in addressing the symptoms of depression; the narrator was specific in his emphasis of this. However, spiritual treatment confronts the ailment at the core of its existence. Once again, a more comprehensive explanation of confronting spiritual enemies is provided in the book, *'Winning Spiritual Wars, Unleashing the Power of the Soul'*. When you are not knowledgeable of the ways that God functions, the enemy uses this to create mythical trigger points that are powerful enough to bring you down naturally and physically. Without knowledge, you will create unrealistic or unsubstantiated expectations of what God will do, as well as what we should do. Unrealistic expectations are what put Elijah in a state of depression. So to defeat depression, we need correct knowledge. Since knowledge is an important weapon for you when confronting depression, it should be clear that the best preparation occurs <u>before</u> the enemy attacks. As a believer, it is important that you know as much as possible about God's plans to establish His kingdom on earth. This is why good, sound, and relative teaching and explaining of God's word is the most effective tool for success against this spiritual enemy. Really, this knowledge is the most effective tool to utilize for success in life.

The next thing that you must do to overcome depression is to **occupy your mind** with positive interactions; get busy doing positive or relative things; things that would normally bring pleasure to you; things that would normally put a smile on your face. I cannot overstate the value of having positive interactions and activities when confronting depression. This enemy of your purpose sets up in your mind and from there seeks to forcefully impact you physically, or forcefully impact your physical environment. Your mind is utilized in every activity that you are involved in, or associated with. You can't conscientiously do a single thing without your mind functioning. We've already discussed the mind, but needless to say that the more time that your mind is occupied with your positive actions, your work, your family gatherings, etc., the less time that there is for depression to work. One thing of importance here that I must note is that alignment with the purpose giver results in a renewed mind[77]. Oh, and one other thing that stood out in that anti-depressant commercial that I mentioned earlier; the actress that was portrayed as the person using their medication to confront the symptoms of depression was active throughout the commercial; always shown

_____

[77] Romans 12;2

participating in a positive activity; their mind was always occupied by what they were doing. A mind that's occupied with positive activities severely limits the amount of time that depression has to perform its evil work. Even your renewed mind should remain occupied with the positive interactions of your life. Growing up, I use to hear the adults frequently say *"an idle mind is the devil's workshop."* Sometimes they would use the word "playground" instead of workshop. But the point is made with either word, and it is a very profound point; the more your mind is used for positive interactions, the less time it is available to attacks of spiritual enemies. Depression is one of those spiritual enemies that want to inhabit your mind. A mind that's centered on the purpose giver will result in peace.[78] A mind that's *"stayed on God"* does not mean that God is all that you think about or all that you do all day every day; it simply means that you have made the purpose giver and His assignment to you a priority. And since He is a priority, you acknowledge Him by doing all that you can to fulfill your Divine Assignment; this you do morally, ethically, compassionately, honorably, and in a way that would be acceptable by Him, or in a way in which He would approve.

I could continue listing enemies of your purpose and explaining how to overcome them, but that would require a much larger space than I have allotted for the pages of this book. But at the very beginning of this chapter, I stated that the enemies of your purpose are numerous; but in this chapter I will only cover a few of them. The finally enemy

---

[78] Isaiah 26:3

of your purpose that you must overcome, and that I will cover in this chapter is '**your will**'. That's right, your will. **What you want to do can become an enemy of your purpose!** When the disciples asked Jesus to teach them to pray, the second request in the prayer that He taught them to pray was "*thy will be done in earth, as it is in heaven.*[79]" The number one priority of God's plan for the world is to establish His kingdom here; then everything that He desires to be done in His kingdom, will be done. But this requires that the inhabitants of His kingdom be committed to carrying out His plan as He has created it. And as previously stated, each and every inhabitant in His kingdom on earth has an assignment; a Divine Assignment.

But also, each and every inhabitant in His kingdom on earth is a uniquely created living soul that has been given the responsibility of choice. Every man, woman, boy, or girl has to conscientiously and willingly accept God and commit to His plan. On the surface, this appears to be a no brainer. The creator of the universe has issued an assignment to you, and it is your choice whether or not you will accept it? The correct answer to the assignment issued should be "Yes Lord", I'll do it. But I reiterate with emphasis, that the influence of sin is a deceptive, powerful, and most compelling force. It will exaggerate the pleasures that are available if you refuse and reject your assignment and follow it. This is nothing new about this and this should be expected and prepared for. After all, Jesus himself was tempted to cast away His purpose, and accept the rewards

---

[79] Matthew 6:10

that the influence of sin offered Him.[80] But Jesus' response showed that He prioritized the plan that His father's plan for the world and He understood the dire consequences of turning away from that plan. In His rejection of the temptation, Jesus displayed both Knowledge of who He was and the power that was within Him. Is not the knowledge of who you are and the power that works within you the very first requirements that were presented as a must have priority when overtaking the enemies of your purpose? Jesus had it, He used it, and because of this, He defeated Satan by overcoming the temptation to walk away from His purpose. If Jesus had to have this knowledge to overcome, so do you.

Consider the story of Moses. I like how the Bible describes Moses. Let's look at how the writer of the biblical book of Hebrews recalled the story of Moses:

> *23. By faith Moses, when he was born, was hid three months of his parents, because they saw he was a proper child; and they were not afraid of the king's commandment.*
> *24. By faith Moses, when he was come to years, refused to be called the son of Pharaoh's daughter;*
> *25. choosing rather to suffer affliction with the people of God, than to enjoy the pleasures of sin for a season;*
> **Hebrews 11:23-25**

---

[80] Matthew 4:1-8

Moses' parents realized at birth that he was a *'proper'* child. By wording it this way, the writer of Hebrews lets us know that Moses' parent recognized at birth, or at an early age, that he was born with a Divine Purpose. But more importantly to this chapter is verse twenty-five. Moses made the choice to fulfill his purpose by choosing to reject the influence of sin, and the pleasures that it offered him. He valued his purpose and his assignment from God to be more valuable than the rewards that were offered him to walk away from his assignment. So Moses' desire, or his will, was to do the work for which he was assigned.

God does not, nor has He ever forced anyone to fulfill their purpose. He makes the assignment and leaves it up to you to fulfill it or not. He lets us know what the benefits are if we chose to accept and fulfill, as well as the consequences if we answer no and refuse. This is why it's important to commit to and align with the purpose giver, then your desires will align with His plan. If I had to provide one solid example from the Bible where a man's will did not line up with God's plan, I would use Jonah.[81] Jonah was given an assignment to go to a certain city and deliver a message to the people there. Jonah didn't want to go because he thought that the people didn't deserve the mercy that he knew God would extend, if they accepted the message. So Jonah did what he wanted to do (*his will*) instead of fulfilling the assignment that he had received from God. He took off going to the city that he wanted to go to; no doubt he would have preached the message to the people there, because he thought that they deserved to hear

---

[81] Jonah chapters 1-3

it. But the results were catastrophic for Jonah. His refusal to accept his assignment from God first resulted in him being adrift at sea in the midst of a Hurricane, then realizing that the storm was because of his disobedience; he was thrown overboard and ended up in the belly of a whale. And from the belly of the whale, Jonah asked the purpose giver for another chance, and he received it. The next time that the purpose giver assigned Jonah to go to that city, Jonah took off towards that city expeditiously! Jonah was given another chance to fulfill his assignment.

What you want to do, or your will, could be a purpose killer, if you are not aligned with and committed to the purpose giver. No one knows the timing of God, or whether you will have another opportunity to fulfill your assignment like Jonah; so when you identify your purpose, you should immediately say yes to the purpose giver, and get to work in the area of your purpose. So many times, we look at the successes of others and then our desires become to do what they are doing in hopes of experiencing the success that we see them experiencing. But that may not be your purpose area. Their assignment may not be your assignment. If you want to experience success, you must first identify your purpose; it is your superpower. Once identified, you must begin fulfilling that assignment. You will learn that you are simply unstoppable when you are functioning in the area of your purpose and fulfilling your Divine Assignment. Then you will know that, without a doubt, your purpose is your superpower!

The take-a-ways from this chapter that you need to retain as you read further in this book are:

1. The enemies of God become the enemies of your purpose once you commit to your assignment
2. Fear keeps you from starting your work in the area of your purpose
3. Fear must be confronted in faith
4. Depression is a spiritual enemy that impacts the natural world
5. Depression comes to force you to quit working in your purpose area after you have started
6. Your mind has dual consciousness
7. Anxiety works with depression
8. Your will can be an enemy of your purpose if you are not in alignment with God
9. Knowledge is used to confront Depression
10. Depression should be treated medically and spiritually
11. God does not force His will on anyone
12. Occupy our mind to fight depression

YOU STILL HAVE TIME

A very good friend of mine often says, *"You can buy a watch, but you can't buy time, so every day that you get is a good day."* No truer statement regarding time has ever been made. Time marches on from day to day, month to month, year to year, decade to decade, century to century, etc. It marches on systematically without showing favor to anyone. Some will miss out on some things, others will be left behind, and yet others will be caught by surprise. Regardless of where time finds you, it continues its unwavering march towards its destiny. It is within this structure of time's inflexible march toward destiny that the purpose giver has devised a master plan for all of humanity. And it is within this structured move towards an expected end, that the purpose giver created an assignment just for you. The purpose giver is also the one who created time, so to devise a plan that's time dependent is but a small part of the master plan.

Remember earlier, I likened God to a Project Manager that's managing a master plan and making individual Divine Assignments to everyone on the earth. But to grasp the fullness of understanding on just how awesome the time management function is for such a plan, consider that the master plan had to be inclusive of every human to populate the earth, from Adam to now, and beyond into the future. This means that every person to ever occupy space on this earth had a unique assignment given to them; an assignment that was specific for a function relating to their time on earth. There is expectation that the assignment given you, was given to be completed within a timeline that corresponds to your time on earth. Solomon put it this way:

1. To every thing there is a season, and a time to every purpose under the heaven:

2. a time to be born, and a time to die; a time to plant, and a time to pluck up that which is planted;

3. a time to kill, and a time to heal; a time to break down, and a time to build up;

4. a time to weep, and a time to laugh; a time to mourn, and a time to dance;

5. a time to cast away stones, and a time to gather stones together; a time to embrace, and a time to refrain from embracing;

6. a time to get, and a time to lose; a time to keep, and a time to cast away;

7. a time to rend, and a time to sew; a time to keep silence, and a time to speak;

8. a time to love, and a time to hate; a time of war, and a time of peace.

Ecclesiastes 3:1-8

This gives a whole new meaning to time management! So God knows our schedule before He brings you into this world. Note in the very first verse that there is a time applied to *"every purpose under the heaven."* Your purpose is included in this. I admit that many times I don't understand why things happen at the times that they happen, but I don't have access to the master plan, therefore I can only trust that the purpose giver has a reason for every action that occurs at preplanned and precise times.

When you perform the life's audit that was a part of the purpose identification process, know that there was a reason why all of those things happened to you at the precise times that they did. You were homeless, living in your car; there was a reason for that to occur at that exact time. You lost a loved one that was your rock when you thought that you needed someone to lean on or else; there was also a reason for that. You lost a child in the process of giving birth; there was a reason for that. You've experienced many horrible and terrible incidents in your life; well, it may be hard to grasp, but there were reasons for that too. I know that some of the things that occurred seemed harsh, but remember that in order to make a desirable omelet; you must start by breaking a few eggs. The purpose giver created a plan and a timeline for your life before your birth. Nothing in your life has happened by coincidence. Nothing just occurred. It was all planned. If we know anything about the purpose giver, we know that He is very detail oriented. It is written that He has numbered the very hairs on your head.[82] He makes sure that even the grass is properly clothed during it tenure on earth.[83] He even makes sure that daily meals are prepared for the sparrows.[84] This is attention to detail; forgetting no one and no relevant thing. It is with this detail that your assignment was created and issued to you upon your arrival into this world. This is why faith in the purpose giver is essential to your success in your assignment. You must have faith that all of these things that you thought were bad,

---

[82] Luke 12:7
[83] Matthew 6:20
[84] Matthew 6:26

were scheduled in your timeline to work for your good. Some things occurred because they were scheduled in your timeline to strengthen you for your assignment. Some things occurred because you stepped off of your purposed path, and God used these things to place you back on path. Many times, the things that were used to place you back on path were not comfortable, or pleasant, but they were effective. Some things happened to create faith in yourself, faith in your unique abilities, faith that will propel you to stardom in your purpose. And still, other things happened to teach you lessons; lessons that you will remember forever and teach to others; lessons that will save lives and create a better existence for others. And I cannot overstate the fact that so many of the bad things that occurred along the path to where you are today were the work of the enemies of your purpose, trying to destroy you before you got started on your assignment. But look at you now. You are here. You are strong. You are full of faith. You are qualified. You've been prepared. You are unstoppable. One look in the mirror reveals that you don't look like what you come through. You look marvelous! No one can say why God put you through the path that He did, but because you are here now, you know that the pain, hardship, troubles, etc. of your past were all in preparation for your purpose. And even when the enemies of your purpose tried to destroy you, the time for you to begin walking in your purpose had not arrived, so God took the enemy's weapon of destruction, and turned it around for your good. And look at you now; things did work for your good after all.

Often, we worry ourselves trying to figure out why? But only the purpose giver can answer those questions; that's why faith in Him is a requirement. Have you ever wondered about God's timeline for your personal purpose? Do you ask questions like "Since God knows what He wants me to do, why didn't He just have me get started years ago?" or "Why did God let this happen to me if He had an assignment for me?" or "Couldn't God have just let me get started on my purpose without having to deal with this?" These are just some of the questions that we ask God, looking back on our timeline. But you should keep in mind that you don't know the specifics of the master plan. Really, you don't even know the specifics of your plan; faith in the purpose giver is a requirement. The late Lashun Pace sang a song entitled "My Times". I love this song because with it she acknowledges that the exacting detail that God used to create His plan for her resulted in the best life for her. She said that had she been in control of her life she would have created a much different plan. She wouldn't have included the hurt, or the pain, or the disappointments. But after seeing the joyous place that God's plan brought her to, she concluded that her plan shows just how little she knew about leading and controlling her life, because all of the things that she would have omitted, ended up working to make the best Lashun Pace. Even though God's plan for her included hurt, pain, and disappointments, all things that she would have omitted had she been allowed to create her own plan, it proved to be the best and correct plan for her in the end. The end justified the means. What an awesome God!

When considering the timing for events on the path leading up to fulfilling one's purpose, no example is more compelling to trust the process than the example of the Apostle Paul.

Paul indicated that his purpose was to be the apostle designated to take the gospel to the Gentiles[85]. But the timing of the fulfillment of his purpose was baffling, even unto Paul. Paul spoke proudly of his birth into a privileged Jewish family of distinction. He talked of his family, a family that were the descendants of Jacob's son Benjamin. He boasted that prior to his conversion; he was a Hebrew of Hebrews. Furthermore, he exclaimed that during that time that he lived a life that was blameless, when considering the law. He was educated by the respected scholar of his day.[86] It would appear that by all standards, he'd be the first in line for selection for discipleship. But when the first disciples were selected, Paul wasn't included.[87] Then when the gospel begin to spread and disciples were being selected in great number, surely Paul would be selected; but no. Instead of being selected then, Paul was out persecuting them that were God selected[88]. Even when Steven testified before the Jewish council, Paul was there, instigating his death.[89] And through all of Paul's religious training, his religious zeal,[90] or his privileged upbringing, he had not been selected for his purpose. Even Paul, looking back on how he began fulfilling his purpose, appeared to be puzzled by the timing. Look at how he described the timing of

---

[85] Romans 11:13
[86] Acts 22:3
[87] Luke 6:13-16
[88] Galatians 1:13; 1 Corinthians 15:9; acts 22:3-4; Acts 26:9-11
[89] Acts 7:58-60
[90] Galatians 1:14

Jesus' appearance to him as compared to His appearance to the other Apostles.

> *"And last of all he was seen of me also,*
> *as of one born out of due time."*
> **1 Corinthians 15:8**

Paul indicated that the timing of his selection to be as one that was born out of due time! WOW! It's so good that Paul's plan was not God's plan. But as Paul begin to fulfill his purpose, he realized that the timing of his selection was all a part of God' plan. This is what he said then.

15. But when it pleased God, who separated me from my mother's womb, and called *me* by his grace,

16. to reveal his Son in me, that I might preach him among the heathen;

Note how Paul has now gone from stating that the timing of him starting his purpose, (*Jesus' appearance to him*) was like a person born out of time, to understanding that he started his purpose when God said it was time for him to start his purpose; and when God said that it was time to start, God's starting time was based on His master plan. And there is nothing untimely about that at all. Paul, like the song that Lashun Pace sang, learned just how little he knew about leading and controlling his life. So all of the time that Paul may have thought that he was ready and should have started fulfilling his purpose, the purpose giver said it's not time yet. My plan calls for you to do these things at these times, and when it is time, I will allow you to begin fulfilling your purpose.

You may not understand why it is taking so long with you. Or you may not know why it took so long with you. But know that God has a master plan and you are in it. There is an open spot in the puzzle and your piece is needed. You have a part in God's plan, and when you begin working on your part, fulfilling your purpose, the superpower in you will awaken.

So wherever you may be reading this, or whenever you are reading this, there is one thing that you need to know. YOU STILL HAVE TIME! Time is a very valuable commodity, but there still is some remaining. So if you haven't identified your purpose and started fulfilling it, God is displaying longsuffering and extending grace unto you, thereby giving you time to get started. If you have already begun fulfilling your purpose, then there is yet more work for you to do. Get started! Keep working! The World is waiting! Your SUPERPOWER is calling! Your SUPERPOWER is needed!

The take-a-ways from this chapter that you need to retain as you read further in this book are:

1. Time waits for no one
2. God's timing is not our timing
3. If you have not identified your purpose and started fulfilling it, then now is the time to get started.
4. If you have already started fulfilling your purpose, the you are yet here because there is still more in the area of your purpose that you must do
5. There are many reasons that the things in your past occurred
6. There is a time for everything in God's plan
7. God is much better at planning your life than you could ever be

APPENDIX

PREDESTINATION

When presenting on a specific topic such as purpose, there are additional knowledge areas that must be clarified relative to the topic. For a topic such as purpose, predestination is such a knowledge area. There is so much confusion and mis-information about this subject, but to understand Divine Purpose, we must also understand predestination.

The Oxford Language Dictionary defines the word 'predestine' as *'determine (an outcome or course of events) in advance by divine will or fate'*. It also states that predestine is a verb, or an action. This would mean that the definition of the word 'predestination' is *'any process where the action of predestinating is applied'*. We have used biblical references in this book to show that every person born into this world was born into God's plan to establish His kingdom on earth, and then given an assignment (purposed) that supports this plan. And further, it has been established that God's plan doesn't predestine anyone to perish. Peter states in 2 Peter 3:9:

> "The Lord is not slack concerning his promise, as some men count slackness; but is longsuffering to us-ward, **not willing that any should perish**, but that all should come to repentance."

Therefore, any assignment that God makes within His plan would result in life for the servant to whom the assignment is made. What this means then, is that everyone born into this world was **predestined for heaven**! God never intended for anyone to perish in Hell; as a matter of fact,

He stated that Hell was created for the devil and his angels (Matthew 25:41).

> **"Then shall he say also unto them on the left hand, Depart from me, ye cursed, into everlasting fire, <u>prepared for the devil and his angels</u>:"**

But we know that many will perish (Matthew 7:13-14).

> **"Enter ye in at the strait gate: for wide is the gate, and broad is the way, that leadeth to destruction, and many there be which go in thereat:**
>
> **Because strait is the gate, and narrow is the way, which leadeth unto life, and few there be that find it."**

So how is it possible for people to go to hell if everyone is predestined for heaven? The answer is in understanding just what predestination means.

Predestination by definition and application addresses and defines the <u>outcome</u> of an event. It establishes that the end result of an action is already set. Predestination does not, however, address the choice of action taken. So in the middle of any road, there are two accessible directions that a person could take. These two directions lead to two different destinations, or in other words, the destination for each direction is pre-determined. Once on that road, going to your right takes you to destination A, and going to your left takes you to destination B: if you want to arrive at destination B, then I can predestine you to B by placing you

103

on that road facing left, then starting you on your journey. Now all along your journey to B, there will be temptations to draw you away from the path that on which you started and take you along another path. If you yield to temptation and take another path, you will arrive at another destination,

EVEN THOUGH YOU WERE PREDESTINED
TO DESTINATION B!

This is what God did for us. In Ephesians 1:11, the Apostle Paul writes:

> **" in whom also we have obtained an inheritance, being predestinated according to the purpose of him who worketh all things after the counsel of his own will:"**

The Apostle Paul teaches that God predestined us according to His plan for the world, which plan we have already shown is to establish His kingdom on earth. So when a baby is born, that baby is birthed into this world and purposed with an assignment in God's plan for this world. The very process of being born into a world where God has stated that He is establishing His kingdom, and everyone in His kingdom will have assignments based on His plan for the kingdom, means that you were born predestined to heaven. The challenge for any of us is the same as it was for Adam in the garden; we must reject the temptations that lure us away from the path that God has established for us.

CCC
Career * Community * Church

This guidance is applicable only after your Divine Purpose has been confidently identified and you are to commit to fulfilling it and living your very best life!

At the heart of the CCC guidance is God's plan for your good, for the good of the local community, and the good of the global community. As the God of everybody, he gives us good for our benefit, and for the benefit of our world. When considering God's supply into our well-being, James so emphatically declares that:

> *"Every good gift and every perfect gift is from above"*
> **James 1:17**

God has always been, He is, and He will always be moving us towards a good that makes us, our community, and the world better.

CAREER

So the first "**C**" represented in the heading of this discourse is for **Career**. You have always been the object of God's affection, and His purpose for you provides the very best for you. Once you identify your purpose, the first place to look to apply your skills should be in support of you. It is a fact that you cannot effectively assist others if you are in need of this same assistance. When you fly on an airplane and the safety instructions are presented over the plane's intercom system, there is a point when they instruct on the proper action to take if the air masks drop from their overhead storage location. The instruction is to first put on your mask so that you can breathe; then put the mask on anyone traveling with you who may need assistance. If you fail to secure your oxygen supply, you will soon find yourself unable to help others secure theirs; YOU MUST TAKE CARE OF SELF FIRST! Your purpose is a part of God's plan for the good of the world; therefore, your part of the plan must start with you. Your purpose will prove to be for the good of you, so that you can then do good for others. Jesus teaches us that we are indeed to love our neighbor, but only as we love ourselves.

> *"Thou shalt love thy neighbour as thyself."*
> **Matthew 22:39**

Fulfilling your purpose within the confines of career and employment can at times be nerve wrecking. You may need to change positions within your company, or maybe you need to go to another company all together. A company with a mission, objectives, and goals that are suitable for your skills. You may even have to become an entrepreneur and begin a function, as many did during the global pandemic of 2020. But you need to know that fulfilling your purpose will bring you success that has been guaranteed by the purpose giver.

> *"Beloved, I wish above all things that thou mayest prosper and be in health, even as thy soul prospereth."*
> **3 John 1:2**

COMMUNITY

The next "**C**" represented in the heading of this discourse stands for community. We are all a part of both a local community, and the global community. As such, when we work to improve our local community, it also improves the global community. We should look for places within our community for purpose fulfillment. Concerning our local community, we are advised:

> *"Now we exhort you, brethren, warn them that are unruly, comfort the feebleminded, support the weak, be patient toward all men. See that none render evil for evil unto any man; but ever follow that which is good, both among yourselves, and to all men."*
> **1 Thessalonians 5:14-15**

Community is important to God. It can be argued that at the very beginning, when God created Adam and Eve and instructed them to replenish the entire earth, His command was for them to create a global community. God has placed within you certain skills for your benefit, but He also desires that you use these skills to assist others.

> *"We then that are strong ought to bear the infirmities of the weak, and not to please ourselves."*
> **Romans 15:1**

Because God has purposed you, and you are strong in the fulfillment of your purpose, then you should use your divinely assigned skills to improve the community in which you live. In this you are doing what pleases the Purpose Giver. It could be that your purpose is assigned for community, in which case your career and community are inter-related such that your prosperity is married to your work for others. NOTE: Serving community takes on many forms. It is not all charity work. You may have a for profit business assisting other business owners, supplying the services that they need. You may be a consultant in one of the many areas where corporations, businesses, etc. function. You may also provide services for the community like construction, counseling, mechanical, etc.

CHURCH
The final "**C**" represented in the heading of this discourse stands for community. There is no doubt that the Church is important to God. Jesus deemed the church as ***God's House*** and the ***House of Prayer*** in one single declaration.

> *"It is written, My house shall be called*
> *the house of prayer;"*
> **Matthew 21:13**

Although there are those who are purposed to function at or in the house of God, God's house was established and purposed for everyone. Jesus called it the 'House of Prayer' and the writer of Hebrews counsels us to make attendance a part of our lives:

> *"not forsaking the assembling of ourselves together, as the manner of some is; but   exhorting one another:*
> **Hebrews 10:25**

It's God's house. It here where we are instructed to submit our prayers, exhort and encourage each other, hear words of direction and guidance from God through the preacher,

> *"and how shall they hear without a preacher?"*
> **Romans 10:14b**

So God has expectations that the 99% of His creation that is purposed with functions not directly associated with His house, would consistently gather in His house for worship. This is an integral part of God's overall plan that we see in implementation even after the New Heaven and the New

Earth are established in Revelation Chapter 21. This third "**C**" also establishes the mechanism through which God's house is provided for, and this is a critical part of God's overall plan for the world.

So, once you identify your purpose, remember the three "**C**"s as you fulfill your assignment and walk in the area of your purpose.

You can schedule Pastor Razor for a Purpose Discovery workshop at www.henryrazorministries.net

Other conferences/seminars/workshops are available at www.fpbi.net

You can connect with Pastor Razor:

Facebook @Henry PastorRazor

Instagram @ pastor_razor

Twitter @ Pastor_Razor